Writing an Essay

If you want to know how . . .

Writing an Assignment

Effective ways to improve your research and presentation skills

Critical Thinking for Students

Learn the skills of critical assessment and effective argument

Make Exams Easy

Time-proven exam techniques that really make a difference to results

Practical Research Methods

Up-to-date ways to master research in six stages

Quick Solutions to Common Errors in English

An A–Z guide to spelling, punctuation and grammar

howtobooks

Please send for a free copy of the latest catalogue to:
How To Books
3 Newtec Place, Magdalen Road,
Oxford OX4 1RE, United Kingdom
email: info@howtobooks.co.uk
http://www.howtobooks.co.uk

Writing an Essay

*Simple techniques to transform
your coursework and examinations*

BRENDAN HENNESSY

4th edition

howtobooks

Published by How To Books Ltd,
3 Newtec Place, Magdalen Road,
Oxford OX4 1RE, United Kingdom.
Tel: (01865) 793806. Fax: (01865) 248780.
email: info@howtobooks.co.uk
http://www.howtobooks.co.uk

First edition 1994
Second edition 1995
Third edition 1996
Fourth edition 1997
Fourth edition revised and updated 2000
Reprinted 2001
Reprinted with amendments 2002
Reprinted 2004
Reprinted 2005

British Library Cataloguing in Publication Data.
A catalogue record for this book is available from
the British Library.

Cartoons by Mike Flanagan
Cover design by Baseline Arts Ltd., Oxford

Produced for How To Books by Deer Park Productions
Typeset by Anneset, Weston-super-Mare, North Somerset
Printed and bound by Cromwell Press, Trowbridge, Wiltshire

Contents

List of Illustrations

Preface
to the Fourth Edition

Students have to write essays at all stages of their education, from pre-GCSE coursework essays of around 500 words to the 2,000 words upwards required for second degrees. It is the most efficient test devised of students' knowledge of their subject, of their ability to think analytically and creatively and to contribute to the subject, and of their ability to communicate their ideas effectively. Yet much guidance is sketchy, especially at tertiary level. Other guides laboriously pick over the innards of a misguided effort at an essay in order to diagnose the diseases, without having first explained what a healthy essay should be like inside, or how you acquire the simpler skills needed for schoolwork and build on them.

My aim has therefore been to fill this gap. There is plenty of self-assessment, so that the student is consistently monitoring progress rather than trying to understand prescriptions couched in academic jargon. This book will be of benefit to students at any stage from age 14 to MA level, with around A-Level as the average pitch of the material.

I believe that those students who begin to use it at 14 will still be benefiting from it in any tertiary courses they take up. By then they will be using it like a computer manual, able to find exactly the bit of advice they need when they get stuck. For I have outlined the principles and shown them in action in as simple and direct a manner as possible. The essential advice doesn't change from one level to the other: the quality and depth of the essay required at different stages will be forthcoming if the skills have been developed and the knowledge obtained.

My approach should also be found welcome by mature students who have returned to formal courses after a period away from them, and who have got out of the habit of essay writing. I have had students from overseas in mind, too.

Self-assessment tasks with suggested responses — descriptions rather than prescriptions — deal with a wide variety of subjects. These range from the more 'creative' schoolroom titles for English to those in various disciplines set by the Boards for GCSE and GCE exams and by

9

universities and colleges of further education. There is something to be learned from working through various kinds and levels.

Case studies at the end of each chapter provide 'real-life essay situations', and also, I hope, a few laughs. We follow the fortunes of six (fictional) students of different levels and abilities as they advance.

My wider aim is to benefit anyone in working life who needs to produce pieces of continuous writing. Collecting and organising information and using it to present coherent expositions and arguments are not the exclusive preserve of the essay. The business report, brochure, advertisement feature and article for newspaper or magazine are among other writing products that require the same basic skills.

I am indebted to the following organisations for permission to reproduce essay titles: ULEAC (University of London Examinations and Assessment Council), the Open University, Oxford Delegacy of Local Examinations and the Southern Examining Group. The sources of these titles are acknowledged in the text. These organisations accept no responsibility whatsoever for the accuracy or method of working in the answers given. Many titles show no acknowledgement: I made them up, and as far as I know they have not appeared elsewhere. I am also grateful to Longman Group for permission to reproduce an extract from G M Trevelyan's *Illustrated Social History*, Vol. 4.

I must thank students for providing some of the samples commented on. Most of the commentary on such samples is my own; some of it has been adapted or added to from commentaries provided by teachers/ lecturers in different disciplines. I must thank them for allowing me to do this without specific acknowledgements.

The Introduction includes a note to the tutor on getting the best out of the book in the classroom. I am glad to hear it has been equally successful as a text for the classroom as for the self-learning student. The book is, of course, designed to meet both requirements.

In this edition I have clarified some points, and as with earlier editions I have responded to the most useful suggestions received.

I shall continue to be grateful for comments on how the book works in practice, from tutors and students. Please write to me c/o the Publishers.

Brendan Hennessy

Introduction

HOW THIS BOOK CAN HELP YOU

This book is a tool that you will adapt to your particular needs and temperament. What are its content and the methods?

1. The emphasis is on practice and self-assessment, with plenty of guidance and suggested responses to the tasks. Special attention has been given to those aspects of essay writing that students say they find hardest.

2. There are numerous examples of how things go wrong and how they can be put right, with commentary, in essays on a variety of subjects. These examples will help you to assess the essays you undertake from now on.

3. You will be constantly asked to review your knowledge and skills as you go. Memory checks within chapters, and three features — case studies, a summary and discussion points — encourage this process.

4. There is no mystery or magic about essay-writing techniques. They can be learned, and I am on your side. Work through this book as suggested, and I promise you that your essays will improve and that you will find the book a useful trouble-shooter in any emergency.

HOW TO USE THE BOOK

- **Read the book straight through** quickly first to get the lie of the land.

- **Read the book carefully**, noting strategies that you specially need. Use the checklists and practical tasks to monitor your progress. If a checklist reveals lack of understanding, read the section again, and test yourself again.

- **Write** your answers to the tasks before comparing with the suggested versions at the back of the book. These versions are not of course intended to be prescriptive. Every essay written on a particular topic is different: what can be assessed is how well or badly it deals with the questions raised by the topic; how well argued it is; how well structured.

- **Adapt** all advice to your own requirements.

- **Repeat** any tasks you have not done well.

- **Revise** sections as necessary when you get stuck in the course of writing an essay.

- **Revise**, when an essay is returned, the sections of the book dealing with the aspects criticised.

- **Identify** when you can with the students meeting the problems in case-studies. These are constant reminders of how to deal with problems as they arise in the essay writing process, including psychological ones.

- **Review** from time to time as you work through the book, using the end-of-chapter summaries. Fill in the details in your mind: if you find this hard, look quickly through the chapter again.

- **Stimulate** your thinking with the Discussion Points, the final section in most chapters. These are open-ended, to encourage you to use your imagination, without the pressure to come up with a 'correct' approach. Tutors may want to use them and add to them in the classroom.

PREPARING FOR EXAMS

Chapter 11 concentrates on the techniques for preparing for and performing at exams. But to provide practice in working at the speed that will be required in exams, time limits are suggested for some of the tasks throughout the book.

- Work to these time limits.

- Revise before exams those sections of the book you have found difficult.

- Do past exams as practice for a month or so before exams.

INTRODUCING THE CASE STUDIES

Neil is a year 11 student

Neil is 16, a year 11 student. His father is a self-made businessman. There are two younger children. Neil starts any task with plenty of enthusiasm but it tends to fizzle out quickly. He lacks self-confidence and he tends to be over-sensitive to criticism; a rather aggressive manner doesn't always succeed in hiding the vulnerability.

His leisure activities include playing and watching football, playing computer games, watching TV, and studying puzzle and magic books.

His main difficulties with essays at present are:

- He produces slapdash work when his interest hasn't been sufficiently aroused.

- He doesn't think hard enough about what the title demands, and doesn't know *how* to think about it.

- He finds the idea of planning boring and prefers to think as he writes. This often works better for 16-year-olds who have not amassed enough knowledge to find comparisons and patterns in it, as long as the students are prepared to scrutinise the result carefully and see what rewriting is necessary. Neil is rarely willing to rewrite.

Marjorie is studying for A-levels

17-year-old Marjorie got seven GCSEs and is now studying four subjects for A-Levels: English Literature, Sociology, Economics and French — at a boarding school. She is an only child of wealthy South African parents. She is well organised, with an incisive mind. She is serious and conscientious.

Her current difficulties are:

- She is a perfectionist, called a 'swot' by her classmates, worries unduly and then doesn't do herself justice.

- She finds it difficult to let her imagination loose when it is demanded.

- She distrusts the emotions. She finds it hard to judge when to stop researching and start writing.

- She finds it hard to maintain a flow and suffers from writer's block.

- She generally learns conscientiously from criticism. But she can be frustrated when she feels a tutor is unaware of the value of what she is trying to express, of what is in her mind.

- She needs to work at producing her own voice and conclusions.

Walter is a computer consultant

Walter is married with two young children. He is a 43-year-old senior computer consultant with a degree in Computer Science. He has a very straightforward, decisive manner. His recreations are DIY about the house.

He has been told that he lacks communication skills — what his company calls 'people skills' — and that further promotion would require from him more reports, memos and correspondence. He has taken the hint, for he is ambitious. As a start he is taking Foundation courses by correspondence in English Literature, History and Political Theory. He expects to follow this up with a degree in History, believing this will humanise him and correct the imbalance towards the sciences in his education.

- He is industrious and when he is determined to accomplish something, he usually succeeds. If he knows something about a subject he can usually produce a satisfactory essay, but he is finding essays in English Literature extremely frustrating.

- He bottles up his emotions and finds it difficult to discuss questions of feeling.

● English Literature essays probe parts of his mind that twelve years in computers haven't reached, and he's not sure if those parts should be disturbed.

● He asks all his tutors for a foolproof method. They say there isn't one foolproof method, that he should try out several methods until he finds one that suits him, and adapt it to different requirements.

Christine is a year 11 student

Christine is 16, outgoing and disorganised. She lives, and goes to the local secondary school, in a deprived inner city area, where she is in year 11. The marriage of her parents is stormy. Home life is noisy, with three younger sisters. She usually works in the sitting room with the family sitting round the TV set. When she has an essay to do she tries to escape to the local reference library.

She has many good points. She has potential, though so far this has not been obvious in her written work. She is beginning to get ambitious, and applies herself more seriously to her studies. She has plenty of ideas and is beginning to produce good creative work.

● She doesn't read as much as she should, and this shows up in a lack of vocabulary. Her English tutor is constantly encouraging her to read more, and she is beginning to respond.

● She tends to be verbose.

● She also has grammar and spelling problems.

● She enjoys class discussion, and is effective.

● She is able to benefit from discussing her essays with friends, and is learning to weigh up different points of view.

David is studying for A-levels

David was born in England 17 years ago of Nigerian parents. His father has an import-export business with branches in Lagos, Hamburg and London, and his mother runs a kindergarten. David is studying A-Levels — Business Studies, English Literature, Law and Government and Political Studies.

His good points are: he is bright, and he researches quickly and effectively. He knows how to organise himself and plan his assignments. He has ideas, is persuasive in argument, and likes to discuss essay topics with fellow-students and members of his family.

● His current problems with essays centre upon being a good starter but a weak finisher. He becomes enthusiastic about a project and that will take him effectively through the shorter kind, particularly in Business Studies. Longer essays, however, he finds a drag and his early interest tends to wane.

● He doesn't take enough notes, and depends on language skill rather than analytical skill to get him through exposition and argument. In other words he can be glib and lacking in substance.

● He tends to leave the writing up to the last minute, and neglects final revising.

● He finds it particularly difficult to come to a conclusion.

Ann is an undergraduate

Studying away from home for a Psychology degree in a country town university, 20-year-old Ann is in her first year. After A-Levels she took a year off to travel in South America. She has an elder brother who has just qualified as an architect. She is an independent spirit, self-assured and energetic. She plays a full part in the social activities of university life, is a frequent speaker in the Debating Society, and is active in student politics. In fact she tends to neglect her studies to fit all this in.

● Her essays both benefit and suffer from her skill at speech making: on the one hand they are interesting and readable; on the other hand they can be repetitive, tending to go round in circles.

● She depends on mind maps for plans, but they tend to become overloaded with detail, and she has been advised to try the detailed formal outline, to keep her ideas under control.

● She tends to have too much preamble at the start of her essays.

● Highly individual, she finds it difficult to take criticism.

SUMMARY

This book's aims

A book cannot write an essay for you, but it can certainly help. This book's aims are to show you how to:

● decide what you want to say
● gather the necessary information and ideas
● think about the structure more clearly
● structure the essay logically and convincingly
● write as well as you can.

Note to tutors

The Memory checks can be turned into oral or written tests for the class as a whole. You will see how to adapt these, as well as some of the Tasks, to the particular projects you are setting up, and how to add to them.

To help students to learn how to evaluate their work, I have found the following method helpful. Photocopy one or two students' essays before correcting them. Give each member of the group/class a copy of an essay to assess. They write their comments. Some of these are read out, and compared, if you like, with your own comments. The guinea pigs then respond (or defend!). Finally there is a class discussion on what has been learnt about assessment, with the main points put up on the board.

1

The Purpose of Your Essay

Decide what you have to say, who your audience is, and then how to communicate it.

WHO, WHAT AND HOW

To write anything — not just essays — you must first decide on the purpose, which includes being quite clear about *who* you are talking to. Then you must decide on *what* you have to say — the content; then *how* you will shape it — the structure. Finally, you must decide on the kind of language you use — the style. Under style we can include presentation: whether to write it by hand or type or word-process it, and how to lay it out on the page.

The process
A piece of writing, then, can be conveniently described under four headings:

P for the **PURPOSE**
C for the **CONTENT**
S for the **STRUCTURE**
S for the **STYLE**

The advantage of using the code-word **PROCESS** is that it puts purpose first.

What does your reader need to know?
If your partner is unknowingly heading for the edge as you walk along a clifftop, would you choose that moment to discuss the view, or ask who should be invited to your sister's wedding? Yet written communications often ignore what the reader *needs to know*, concentrating instead on what the writer wants to say.

IDENTIFYING YOUR PURPOSE AS A WRITER

Comparing the techniques needed for different kinds of writing, and practising them, improves writing skills for any purpose. We all have important kinds of writing to do in the course of our lives. Practising these skills (writing a letter rather than telephoning, for example) will make it easier to write essays. Writing essays will prepare us for other writing tasks in our future careers. For this reason we will sometimes compare essay techniques with those required for other 'writing products'.

Comparing the purposes of different kinds of writing will help to make the purpose of the essay clearer by putting it into perspective.

Writing personal letters

The personal letter may have various purposes and may be loose and rambling. It is often a substitute for conversation, discussing matters of interest only to sender and recipient. It may contain private references to shared experience that would not be understood by anyone else. But writing letters encourages your ideas to flow readily, a crucial requirement for a good essay.

In any case there are more formal varieties of letters, which appear among the creative essay choices in GCSE exam papers. Their main purpose is to let you show that you can communicate effectively, with less emphasis on knowledge or structure.

For example:

A friend is thinking of trying to take up a career in music and has written to you asking for advice. Write a letter in reply which does not discourage your friend, but makes clear the difficulties and challenges to be faced *(SEG, GCSE, November 1990)*.

Some of these letters are based on extracts from literature and journalism, which you have to read first.

Writing business letters

These have a specific purpose: to inform, order or sell, so that the sender's business will benefit. Anything irrelevant to its purpose will work against it. A letter asking for a long-standing bill to be paid, after many previous letters and phone calls, will refer to possible legal action rather than inject humour with an apt quotation from Shakespeare.

Writing a business or investigative report

This has its purpose clearly stated, in relation to the content and the readers aimed at. The purpose is the essential part of what is usually titled the Introduction. It may be given the title **Terms of Reference**. The 'terms' are the reasons for the investigation, the situation or problem, the audience, and what action, if any, they are expected or advised to take. The Introduction may include a Summary and Conclusions.

The straightforward patterns and style of such reports work well for certain kinds of essays, especially in the sciences. The outlines of an essay and an investigative report on a similar theme are placed side by side for comparison (see Appendices B and C).

The newspaper report

This aims to state as concisely and objectively as possible the

who	where	why
what	when	how

of any event considered newsworthy, bearing in mind the readership of the publication. This 'Five-Ws-plus-How' formula is a useful reminder of the questions that any piece of writing may be required to answer, including business-style reports and essays, in which we shall see it at work.

The newspaper reporter also aims to be **readable**, but **clarity** is more important. The essence of the news report is often put first, with less important facts filling it out.

The feature articles of newspapers and magazines

These have various purposes. What they have in common is the aim to

inform	explain	entertain
comment	persuade	

and often all five at once. Averaging 600 to 2,000 words, feature articles may explain the background to the news or develop an argument. They usually have a topical peg of some kind.

The personal column or opinion piece is akin to the creative essay of the schoolroom. The following topic, and many similar ones, have been the subject-matter of many a column:

'Modern gadgets!' Give your views on the importance to everyday life of computers, cellular telephones, microwave cookers and satellite television *(SEG, External Syllabus, GCSE, November 1990).*

The main difference between feature articles and essays is that the essay does not have to interest a great number of people, nor does it need to be quite so informative or up to date as the journalism. But both articles and essays have to support opinions with fact.

● As a model for creative essays, study how this support is given in the more subjective personal columns.

● As a model for the more academic essay, the main subject of this book, study how this support is given in articles of exposition and argument.

TASK 1

Find a feature article in a newspaper or magazine. Explain its purpose in 20 words.

Group: A feature article is photocopied and distributed to members of a group. The 20-word reports are compared and discussed.

Writing essays

What is your tutor looking for?

Essays too have their own specific requirements. Tutors normally spell these out to their students, but check with your tutor (or examination body) if you are in any doubt. In general, your essay should show that you can:

● collect relevant information quickly and use the knowledge to focus clearly on the set topic
● read critically and purposefully
● analyse processes and problems and argue a case
● relate theory to specific examples
● make a creative contribution to the subject
● structure the material logically and express it clearly.

Although clarity in essays is more in demand than readability (except for the more creative ones), put yourself in the place of a tutor or examiner who has to wade through a hundred or so in a week. Make your essay as readable as possible without straining for effect. The best journalism will provide models for this quality too.

Letters, reports and articles are often asked for in the 'composition' section of secondary school exams rather than 'essays', and coursework projects take these and other forms.

CASE STUDIES

Neil doesn't quite convince

Neil, reasonably satisfied, took the first paragraph of his coursework project on 'Should the Monarchy be Abolished?' to his tutor:

> 'The country being in its present state of recession can't afford the monarchy. The various castles and palaces cost millions to maintain and that money comes out of our taxes. In any case the Queen is only a figurehead and doesn't have any real power so what's the point? We're in Europe now anyway and don't do so much trade with the Commonwealth, which is supposed to be one reason for keeping it because the Queen is Head of the Commonwealth. The behaviour of the younger members of the Royalty just let the country down and in any case their marriages are split up and that is messing up the whole idea of the monarchy, after all it's supposed to give the country unity. Some people say the tourists come to see the palaces and the Crown jewels and all that, but how many of them are going to see the Queen on a white horse?'

Tutor comment

His tutor asked, 'How does it go on from there?' Neil said he wasn't sure but he would give more details on those points.

The tutor reminded him that his main purpose was to convince readers of his arguments, not just mention them in passing. The remark about the tourists was irrelevant: the contribution of the monarchy to income from tourists had to be answered.

'Look at your materials pack. There are poll figures showing loyalty to the Queen. You've got to weigh arguments for the monarchy against yours. What about the polls in the USA saying that American tourists would come just the same if there were no monarchy? That would support your argument on this point better. . . First make a plan. Take the different aspects: the matter of respect, the Commonwealth, tourism, and so on, and put for and against under each.'

'By the way,' Neil said, 'I wouldn't just stop it of course. I'd phase it out after the Queen.'

'Well, you'd better explain that part of it. Probably in the first sentence.'

Marjorie learns to illustrate with examples

Marjorie is discussing with her tutor the following essay:

> Write about the way the protagonist of *Jane Eyre* develops during the novel and discuss how Charlotte Brontë reveals the development.

Tutor: You've got too much of the social background in, haven't you? Look for the main theme. A rebellious child grows to a mature woman of some strength of character. Then see how she moves towards this at each stage of her development. What are the stages?

Marjorie: Well, she was a rebellious child to some extent when brought up by her aunt, and also at boarding school. But she learns Christian tolerance there from her friend. She goes to Rochester as a governess and falls in love. That's the big deal. She visits her aunt and turns the tables if you like, asserts herself doesn't she? Then back to Rochester, almost marries but hears of bigamy. Runs away, holes up with the Rivers family and almost marries the parson Rivers but it would have been out of duty, reasserts herself and goes back to Rochester. House destroyed, he's blind and lame, cor she doesn't half pile it on here, and then she's going to look after him. A real weepie.

Tutor: What about the question of Charlotte Brontë *revealing*?

Marjorie: But what does it mean exactly, reveals?

Tutor: What the question wants you to do is to illustrate with some examples the advances, the key changes for Jane. Some of the advances are in Jane's mind, in her thoughts, the way she argues with herself, and so on, and of course we see everything through Jane's mind. Some advances are symbolic — think of their first meeting when he comes off his horse and leans on her, and then the tree that splits in the storm and so on. Some advances are revealed in her discussions — with Rochester and with Rivers. It's all psychological isn't it?

Marjorie: Sir, I'm going to study Psychology at university. I find it fascinating.

Tutor: Well, *Jane Eyre* is a good place to start, isn't it?

Walter struggles with his plan

Looking over his essay on 'How to lose weight and keep it lost' for his Foundation course, Walter's head was spinning. It was 2,000 words long. He had not made a plan of it because it had all been clear in his head. Now he saw that he had lost his way in the middle. He made a plan of the structure that he found. The five steps for losing weight were first listed, which was a great help:

1. Decide exactly how much weight you want to lose.

2. Take actions to achieve it.

3. Analyse results of actions.

4. Continue actions if succeeding, or try other methods.

5. Among other methods, find someone who has achieved success and follow that example.

The main problem was step 2. This divided into *actions in general:* first, become interested in your health; secondly, find out where your diet is going wrong; thirdly, get excited about losing weight — take the pleasure rather than the pain. Then there were three *specific actions*, but it was not clear to what general action they referred — all or the last. The third specific action was followed, with no link, to: 'Perhaps you have problem food.' There was a three-step procedure for cracking this type of problem. Step one was to get leverage. Then there were two steps to achieve leverage . . .

Walter asked his tutor how to deal with this.

Tutor comment

'First of all, this is a report rather than an essay, isn't it?' said the tutor. 'I would have advised you to use plenty of headings and bullet points, to avoid this confusing repetition of "steps" and "stages" and "actions". Use "steps" for the five main sections only. Avoid "stages" and keep to "methods", not "actions".

'Your section 2 needs restructuring. This is really the body of the essay. The five points of the procedure should, I think, be the introduction, to explain the whole thing. Then go through the different operations without dividing them further, in the best order. Make sure you link each operation to the next, showing the logic of your order.

'Your essay sounds like someone working at a computer, following up different options to see where they lead you. The computer knows exactly where you're at, but your reader doesn't.'

Walter Jeffrey said, 'Now I wonder why that should be?'

TASK 2 (20 minutes)

In about 50 words for each case, say what each student in the case studies learns about keeping to the purpose.

SUMMARY

To produce an effective piece of continuous writing, you must:

- first identify the purpose
- decide on the content
- plan
- collect information
- draft
- write and rewrite as necessary.

You can improve your essay writing techniques by:

- studying the techniques used in other kinds of writing
- practising those techniques
- adapting them for essays.

Identify the specific requirements for your essay by:

- checking with your tutor
- checking with the examination body.

2

Choosing Your Topic

'The difficulties and disagreements . . . are mainly due . . . to the attempt to answer questions, without first discovering precisely *what* question it is you desire to answer.' G E Moore, *Principia Ethica*, 1903.

To do yourself justice, try to choose the topics that will enable you to make the most of your knowledge and skills. This chapter aims to help you do that. Firstly, remind yourself of the requirements of an essay.

Memory check

Jot down the requirements of an essay – the proofs of your abilities that an essay might be expected to show. Compare your list with that given on page 21.

UNDERSTANDING THE TITLE

'Marry in haste, repent at leisure' applies to choosing essay titles. Make sure you know what is wanted. First use common sense to grasp what the title as a whole expects.

My First Day at Secondary School

This has no instructional word, but you can take it to be 'tell the story of' or 'describe' or 'give your memories of'. Would you simply recount the main events in chronological order? No — you would describe your memories and feelings as vividly as possible; you would bring to life your fellow-pupils and teachers, try to show why your memories are significant, and perhaps reflect on what they tell you about yourself.

Answer the question

The most common fault in essays is *failure to answer the question* — to do what the title requires. In exams this failure may be a result of nerves. Anxiety to complete the exam in time may mean the question is not given the calm consideration it needs. But the term essay can also go off the point unless the question is both analysed carefully and constantly referred to.

Example
Consider this topic:

> Argue the case against the banning of corporal
> punishment of children

Students who are against corporal punishment are liable to answer the wrong question — to argue the case, in other words, against corporal punishment. The topic requires exactly the opposite! The double negative 'against/banning' becomes 'for' corporal punishment.

> Refute the arguments that are made in favour of
> capital punishment

is a title that might similarly lead astray: the positive words 'in favour of' can blur the negative effect of 'refute'.

Note that for neither of the above argument topics does it matter what your view is. You are not judged by your view, only by how well you **argue a particular case**.

KEEPING YOUR TITLE IN VIEW

Misunderstanding can be avoided by constant reference to the topic.

- Write the title as a heading to your work at every stage — notes, plan, first draft, final version.

- Put the topic title on a card and display it above or on your desk.

- Paraphrase it, and if you're not sure that you've got it right, check with your tutor or fellow-students.

Paraphrasing the title

Example

> Argue the case against the banning of corporal
> punishment of children

could be paraphrased as: 'What are the arguments against making it illegal to give corporal punishment to children?' or: 'What are the arguments for keeping it legal to give a reasonable amount of corporal punishment to children?'

An erroneous paraphrase would be: 'What are your views on whether or not corporal punishment of children should be made illegal?' It is not so much *your* views, as *one side of the argument* that must be focused on. Worse would be: 'What do you think about giving corporal punishment to children?' The crucial question of legality has disappeared.

In an exam, write the topic at the head of your essay: it is your title. Again, paraphrase it carefully if it could easily be misinterpreted.

Getting the question clear

When the topic is not expressed as a question, turn it into one. Here is another example:

> 'People don't seem to realise that it takes time and effort and preparation to think. Statesmen are too busy making speeches to think.' Bertrand Russell. Discuss with reference to EITHER Harold Macmillan OR Harold Wilson.

A suitable way of turning this into a question would be, 'How accurately do you think Russell's statement applies to the career of. . .?'

Then work out more questions to guide your reading, devoting a page or two of your notebook to them. Start question-making as soon as you can after receiving your assignment. Add questions that arise in the course of your reading.

● What exactly did Russell mean by 'think'?

● How accurately does his statement apply to politicians generally?

● What were Macmillan's merits and defects as a thinker?

● What contribution did he make to his scripted speeches?

● Did he write many himself?

These are some of the questions that might suggest themselves:

Memory check

In about 12 to 15 words for each, write three examples of essay questions that might lead students astray if they didn't take care to analyse it.

Use for the first: 'Argue the case against . . .'

For the second, use: 'Refute the arguments that are made in favour of . . .'

Find your own formula for the third. Try them out on your colleagues to see if they fall into the trap. Compare your answer with the discussion at the top of page 27.

Questioning the assumptions of the title

You might start to question Russell's assumption: Isn't the way a statesman thinks, you might argue, as worthy of the name as the more sedentary, philosophical kind?

But common sense would bind you to the topic. You would still treat the quotation with respect and concentrate on applying it. Indicate clearly in the essay where you stand, and why. If totally at odds with the assumptions of a topic, you would be wise to choose another one.

Carry a notebook around. You may get ideas from anywhere — from radio, TV, conversations . . .

UNDERSTANDING KEY TERMS AND INSTRUCTIONS

We have been seeing the topics as a whole, considering what they are all about. Looking at the topics more closely you can see two or three different elements:

- **Key terms, or concepts**. These indicate what area of subject-matter your essay should cover.

- **Instructional words**. These tell you what to do with the subject-matter — explain it, compare/contrast it, discuss, argue a particular case or refute it, and so on.

- **Other pointers** to the meaning of the topic: for example, the many varieties of phrases that indicate your opinion is wanted: 'how far . . . to what extent . . .' and so on.

Interpreting key terms

Let us take these in order. What are the key terms in the punishment topic? They are:

'banning'
'corporal punishment'
'children'.

Banning has a clear enough meaning. Can there be doubt about what the other two terms mean? Well, yes, there can! Take corporal punishment: when does a nudge become a tap, a tap become a smack, a smack become a blow, a blow become an assault? If you are doing the essay you have to decide exactly where corporal punishment begins — and also where it turns into physical abuse, because that is another question.

When you start thinking about this, you realise that the age of the child comes into it, too. So you have to define 'children'. Is the school-leaving age, around 16, for example, the upper limit? How much force, at different ages, constitutes 'corporal punishment'? Wait a minute. *Who's* doing it? Should the rules for corporal punishment be the same for parent, nanny, child-minder and teacher — or different?

You can see that by analysing the terms of the topic in some detail, you are well on the way to a good plan for the essay.

General and specific meanings of terms
Use a dictionary to help you define a concept, but do so with caution. Be careful to consider not only the context of the topic but the discipline. 'Poverty' may be a straightforward term in most topics. But in socio-logical essays, when talking about poverty you normally consider the different approaches of theorists, with their varying definitions: from those who tend to see it as caused by individuals' problems, to those (for example Marxists) who see it as the product of a political system.

In literature, you have to be on the alert for terms carrying their contem-porary meaning when the current meaning is different. A quotation may contain words carrying an original meaning some distance from its present day meaning. Here are a few examples (original meanings on the right):

addiction	inclination
conscience	knowledge
illness	ruthlessness
verbatim	orally

It is useful to underline the key terms in a topic. For example:

<u>Argue</u> the case <u>against</u> the <u>banning</u> of <u>corporal punishment</u> of <u>children</u>.

TABLE OF INSTRUCTIONS

Instruction	What it means
analyse	discuss in detail, examine, criticise, review
appraise	evaluate, find the value of
assess	weigh up, judge
compare	find similarities and differences between
contrast	indicate the differences between
criticise	give your assessment of merits and defects
define	give the precise meaning of
discuss	examine in detail, argue, give reasons for and against
describe	give a detailed account, discuss
examine	investigate, scrutinise, discuss
explain	account for, give reasons for, make clear
indicate	point out, show
illustrate	explain with examples
interpret	explain the meaning of
judge	give your opinion/conclusion
justify	give reasons for, show to be true or reasonable
outline	give main points, showing structure, omitting details
refute	prove a statement/argument to be false
relate	make the connections clear between facts and events
state	present simply and clearly
summarise	give a brief account of the main points
trace	show the development of, in clear stages

TASK

Complete in 15 minutes

(a) Underline the key terms in the following topics. Indicate which is the instructional word, supplying it if it isn't explicit.

(b) Paraphrase each topic.

1. 'Wisdom is wasted on the old.' How far do you agree with this statement? *(The 'creative' type, more likely to be set at GCSE Level.)*

2. Why were Allied Forces able to make rapid progress in their North African campaigns during 1942-3 but slow to make progress in their Italian campaigns of 1943-5? *GCSE Modern World History, June 1993 (ULEAC).*

3. What may be the effects of an increase in leisure time? *GCSE, Sociology, June 1993 (ULEAC).*

4. Examine the significance of Brutus's role in Shakespeare's *Julius Caesar.*

5. Does the increasing popularity of fringe religious groups indicate that secularisation is a myth? *A-Level Sociology, May 1983 (Oxford).*

Note that words can vary considerably in meaning according to the context, so use a dictionary with care. The table of instructions on page 31 will be a useful guide to meanings of these.

CASE STUDIES

Christine needs a well-linked argument

Christine has written an essay called 'Cars should be banned from city centres.' Her tutor asks her to read out the first paragraph:

> Conditions in the cities are getting steadily worse. The increasing amount of traffic on the road. Something has to be done to remove cars from the city centres. Cars tend to pollute the air, cause congestion in the city centres, and are not very safe for both pedestrians and people living in and around these centres. As a result of this life is almost always at a standstill during the rush hour.

Tutor comment
The tutor asked: 'What did you mean by "not very safe"?'
    'I meant because of the pollution.'
    'That isn't clear from the sentence, is it? And why not just say that pollution damages the health of city dwellers? That would include the drivers, and all the other people around. Notice by the way, that "The increasing amount of traffic on the road" is not a complete sentence. You should have talked first about the congestion and life being at a standstill. Then about the pollution, which is made worse by the standstill. Read the next paragraph, Christine.'

> The government is doing very little about these problems. The introduction of double yellow lines, red routes, traffic wardens and towing away cars is doing very little to stop the heavy flow of cars into the cities. The government should introduce an effective road and rail system, whereby people will leave their cars at home and use public transport. . .

    'You're arguing better, Christine, but you need to link up the argument more clearly. You haven't mentioned banning yet. Start with your viewpoint — complete or partial banning. Then indicate what your argument is going to be, briefly. One, the chaos of the city centres. Two, the inadequate efforts to deal with it . . . central government and local government. Three, what you think should be done: what effects banning them from the centres would have.'

David is introduced to crisis points
David is about to embark on: 'How does Celie's character change from oppressed teenager to independent woman through *The Colour Purple*?'
    The book tells a story of poor blacks in the southern United States at the turn of the century. He asks his tutor what is meant exactly by '*how?*'.
    Tutor: How? It's not quite the same as *indicate* the changes. It's *illustrate* the changes, explain with examples. Can you give me the stages?
    DA: Well, there are so many. Her stepfather treats her as a slave, and then rapes her. She hasn't got any idea she can complain, and it's the same when she is given to a husband who treats her just as badly. . .'
    Tutor: What's the first real breakthrough into some self- esteem?
    DA: She realises she's worth something when she falls in love with her husband Albert's old flame Shug Avery. I'd have to go through the book again to find the main ones. I should have made notes. Of course

at the end she comes into money and starts a business, and is seen to be stronger than her husband.

Tutor: It's useful to make notes when you've got a fairly long work, because you can waste a lot of time diving into the book to look for passages you vaguely remember. Scan through the book again, this time noting Celie's crisis points. Where she actually moves forward, *changed* in some way. Make notes of these parts. Include in your notes *who* helps her develop, and *what* helps her, because you've got to explain.'

David made notes as suggested. He found two or three crisis points that hadn't remained clearly in his mind. This was a turning point for David as well. He began to make notes on literature more carefully, always looking for the crisis points in novels and plays and how they related to the theme.

Ann is asked to end better

For a one-off certificate course in Science and Technology 1876-1950 Ann has written an essay in response to the question 'How accurately does the label "New Electric Age" characterise changes in everyday life between 1870 and 1950?' Her first paragraph ran:

> The label "New Electric Age" is a generalisation about changes in everyday life between 1870 and 1950. It is used to describe an "average" person's everyday life between 1870 and 1950, but it is meaningless without putting the sampling population and deviations from it into context. In other words, to assess the validity of the label we need to look at whose lives were being described and how they were affected. It is also worth looking into who thought up the label and into the assumption behind it that science and technology would inevitably and increasingly give people a better life.

The body of the essay described the different aspects of life affected, industrial and domestic. The essay ended:

> This label was created by scientists, technologists and entrepreneurs to promote the use of electricity. The ideology behind this label was that electricity technology would bring mankind a better and brighter future.

Tutor comment
'Your conclusion doesn't follow from the good analysis, Ann,' her tutor said. 'You needed to return to the question and show how the different

points you've made do add up to an argument. *How* accurately? And exactly how does that ideology you mention relate to the question? You didn't actually deal with it in the essay, and it needed to be discussed. It's promising, though. I like the way you get straight into it without your usual preamble.'

'This time I've put the preamble at the end,' said Ann.

Her tutor was relieved to see that she was smiling.

SUMMARY

To choose a topic wisely, make sure you understand the title. These are the chief stages in the process of choosing:

- Decide if you are interested enough to live so long with it.

- Use common sense to grasp what the title expects, seeing it as a whole.

- Is the time, and are the books/documents and other sources, readily available?

- Study the title closely and avoid answering the wrong question.

- Paraphrase the title as an aid to understanding it.

- Check your paraphrase with fellow-students and/or tutor.

- Underline and interpret the key terms: note what they mean *in context*.

- Identify the *instructions*, and other pointers to what is wanted.

- Decide how far you agree with the title's assumptions.

3

Collecting the Information You Need

'Knowledge is of two kinds. We know a subject ourselves, or we know where we can find information upon it.' Dr Samuel Johnson.

IMPROVING YOUR RESEARCH SKILLS

The aim of this chapter is to help you master the chief research skills. These are:

● organising your time

● relating the research to the topic

● knowing where to find out

● knowing how to use a library

● reading purposefully

● organising notes.

ORGANISING YOUR TIME

Make sure you meet the tutor's deadline. A late essay may not be accepted. If it is accepted, there may be a deduction of marks. Give yourself a timetable, working back from the deadline. Indicate the dates when you will need to:

● start writing up the final version

● start writing the first draft

● start thinking about the topic purposefully and making an essay plan

● do any interviewing and do the note-taking from printed sources; deciding on the priorities

● make a preliminary survey of sources that the topic demands.

RELATING YOUR RESEARCH TO THE TOPIC

The title of your essay must be constantly referred to while researching so that you collect the information you need — a little more than you need, so that you can select the most relevant, but not so much that you are bogged down or slowed down.

We have seen how out of the question of the title (see page 28), you can formulate a few of your own questions to be answered; these will guide your research.

Example

Let's take a title already paraphrased:

What may be the effect of an increase in leisure time?

would divide into such questions as: what changes will there be to:

1. the way society is ordered?

2. its institutions?

3. the way people live and work?

4. the educational system?

5. the entertainment industries?

First discover what ideas you may have in your mind. List them under each question. You may want to stimulate your thinking by using some kind of brainstorming method (see pages 51–55).

KNOWING WHERE TO FIND OUT

Library research

This means using all kinds of printed sources: books, booklets, magazines, newspapers, pamphlets, publicity materials, and so on.

You may have been given book lists by your tutor: perhaps one for the course and additional lists for each essay topic. Consult your tutor if you need help in selecting.

Books may also be suggested during lectures and tutorials. You may be expected to add to any reading lists provided for essay topics: in other words part of the test may be to show research skills. Look at the

bibliographies listed under encyclopedia entries on your subject. Look at the bibliographies provided in the books on your reading list.

Knowing how to use a library

Use a fairly large reference library regularly and get to know the librarian. You may have quickly learned where the various reference books are and how to use **microfiche catalogues** and **computerised databases**. But when you find sources for a particular essay hard to find, a friendly librarian may save you much time.

Legwork

This means finding out by using your legs and eyes. Go there and see for yourself (an old people's home, a football match).

Live research

This means research by interviewing. The quickest way to get the latest information on a current social problem may be to research like a journalist. You could, for example, interview the director or press officer of a voluntary association (pressure group); armed with their literature, you will be guided to the most recent articles published on the subject.

Other 'experts' might be interviewed. An essay on prisons, for example, might benefit from interview with an official of NACRO (National Association for the Care and Rehabilitation of Offenders), a prison governor or an ex-prisoner.

You will probably have formulated your interview questions during your reading, so that they are informed questions, relevant to your topic: questions that the printed sources have not, as far as your can gather, answered fully or have not yet caught up with. Surveys and questionnaires need to be prepared carefully to produce valid results — a skill that is learned as part of sociology and related courses.

Broadcast media and film

Check through the listings sections in newspapers and magazines to see if there are any programmes relating to the subject of your current project. Videos can sometimes be obtained from organisations publicising their activities.

READING PURPOSEFULLY AND TAKING NOTES

A common formula for an effective reading method is SQ3R:

S is for Sample

Q is for Question

R is for Read

R is for Recall

R is for Review

Sampling a book

The **sampling** or **surveying** procedure is used to see whether a book is suitable for your essay purpose. It involves looking at the:

title
author
date of publication
blurb
contents page
main headings
index
illustrations
preface or introduction.

Question

Study the book in more detail. You will probably read the first and last paragraph of each page. What are the author's aims and how far are they achieved? Question the author's methods and ask yourself if you agree with the author's conclusions.

Read

You are now ready to read the book in more detail. Nevertheless, you may want to do this in two stages: first **skimming** or **scanning**, second **in depth**.

- **Skimming** means quickly exploring the ground covered, noting how the book relates to your essay topic.

- **Scanning** means that you know exactly what you want. You search for the sections dealing with your concerns and ignore the rest.

- **In depth** means reading the relevant sections as slowly as necessary to understand, questioning critically as you go.

There are study guides that help you to check your reading efficiency and to read faster. You may want to prepare for note-taking as you read by putting notes in the margin of your own books, or on photocopied material, or by underlining or highlighting parts of the text.

It is best to read quickly through a text before note-taking, so that you see what is essential. Time can be wasted taking too many notes, and they can defeat the purpose of note-taking. Notes taken from a long text normally need to have page numbers or section headings indicated.

Recall

Recall and **review** are what you do when you meet a memory check in this book. You will improve your memory by regular recalls, at the end of each chapter or section. Recall orally or in writing.

Oral recall

For oral recall get a fellow-student to ask you factual questions on the text. As each answer is approved, write it down.

Written recall

For immediate written recall, first write the marginal notes and do the underlining as described above if not already done. (If the text cannot be marked, do this preliminary note-taking on a sheet of paper.) Study these preliminary notes. Then cover them and reproduce them, fleshing them out as necessary.

Review

Go back through the text quickly. Add to your notes anything important you have left out. At a later stage, just before an exam perhaps, or just before handing in an essay, you will probably want to repeat this review, and you may then find one or two more gaps in your notes.

Memory check

Close the book and explain the SQ3R reading method to your class or a fellow-student, who will be following the text and will prompt you if necessary.

PRACTISING NOTE-TAKING

Practise taking notes from different kinds of texts so that you develop your techniques. Using quality newspaper leaders is recommended: their subject-matter will be varied and styles will be varied. You will find in many a mix of narrative, description, exposition and argument. Choose clear, straightforward leaders. Before attempting the following task, study the sample of note-taking shown in Appendix B.

TASK

Open a quality (broadsheet) daily newspaper at the leader page.

1. Skim-read the first leader, numbering each paragraph and giving it a heading.

2. Then read it in-depth, underlining the main points and listing them in the margin by placing (a), (b), (c), and so on alongside them.

3. Scan-read to fix the main points and the structure in your mind.

4. Close the newspaper and write down your notes of the leader in this schematic form.

5. Check with the leader to see if you have left out any important points.

6. See Appendix B for model and turn to page 164 for further advice.

DECIDING WHAT AND HOW TO NOTE

Your course outline

For all disciplines you should make a **course outline**. You may have been given one by your tutor. Expand this into a larger framework so that when taking notes you will see where they fit into the course as a whole. Make notes on the jargons and on the formulae for different disciplines.

Making a bibliography

Make a **bibliography** of all books and other printed sources consulted. It is useful to indicate briefly for each reference the value of the book for course and essay purposes; show what notes were taken, in case you may want to go back to the book later on.

Notes from books

Note chapter headings of books you may want to study more fully at a later stage. Use the indexes to guide you through a book where the

COMBAT ← ASPECT OF SUBJECT

Barriers against women soldiers ← NOTE IN OWN WORDS

taking combat or combat
related jobs — but combat
experience necessary for top jobs
[Catch 22 situation well summarised] ← STUDENT'S COMMENT

Susan H. Greenbery et al. 'The New ← AUTHOR
Face of Battle,' Newsweek, 10.9.90,
P. 21 ← TITLE, PUBLICATION, DATE, PAGE NUMBER

6" x 4" Note card: note from magazine article

COMBAT

GREENBERY, SUSAN H. ET AL

'The New Face of Battle'
Newsweek, 10.9.90
[Notes taken on barriers
against women.]

5" x 3" Bibliography card: magazine article

WOMEN IN THE ARMED FORCES

MUIR, KATE.
Arms and the Woman

First published Sinclair-Stevenson,
1992 London: Coronet Books, 1993
[Interviews women all ranks W. Forces
— notes taken 15.4.93]

5" x 3" Bibliography card: book

Jargon   pacification

(military) often means
oppressing rather than literal
'making peace'

5" x 3" Jargon/formula card

42

information you need is scattered. Put page numbers or chapter section headings alongside notes taken in case you need to check later: always check quotes (what people have said) and quotations (literary references).

Different disciplines make different note-taking demands. Most require you to collect your own thoughts/reactions as you research. You may want to add, especially for long projects, your immediate reactions to details noted. Such details may include facts that you believe are false and will want to check, and opinions you believe are erroneous. Insert your own thoughts/reactions in square brackets so that they won't be confused with others' opinions. Or you may want to include suitably labelled notes for a future project.

For literature, history, politics and other subjects, a narrative summary may provide a convenient framework, with the important events, periods and stages given dates.

Notes from other sources

Whatever sources of information are used, it is easy to get it wrong. Practising note-taking in the way described above – always checking back with the original – will alert you to any careless reading, thinking and interpreting habits you may have developed. Take notes from newspapers and magazines with special care, and find time to check with at least one other source.

A newspaper report may be flawed in various ways. Lack of time and space means that the selected facts add up to an incomplete picture. Facts may be omitted through a reporter's prejudice, conscious or unconscious, or because of the paper's political leaning. A National Front organ may play down the racism in a particular area. Be on the alert for opinion presented as if it were news.

Study feature articles in newspapers and magazines with an eagle eye for factual errors and flaws in argument. Don't assume that books must have the facts correctly. If in doubt, express your doubt. Better still, check against another source.

Testing for reliability

Are the facts adequate to support the opinions expressed? Are the arguments convincing? Are they weakened by political bias or other kinds of faulty reasoning? There is more in Chapters 6 and 7 on how to think straight and argue clearly, and how to recognise faulty reasoning in your own arguments, in those you meet in discussion with classmates or colleagues, or in your reading.

Take notes in your own words. Repeating chunks of other writers' work in an essay is very noticeable. It shows that you haven't formed your own ideas about the subject matter. Put quote marks around passages you want to quote as evidence. More on this in Chapter 6. When taking notes from lectures and interviews, ignore ramblings and write down only the essential points. Practise with tape-recordings of talks, then play them back to see what you have missed.

The visual-minded may prefer to take notes in diagrammatic forms (**mind maps** are described in Chapter 4).

ORGANISING YOUR NOTES

How elaborately you organise notes is a personal matter, but the following arrangements are recommended for university level if not before. Try them, and make short cuts where you feel you can.

1. Labelled folders containing various materials, including brochures, leaflets, newspaper cuttings and photocopied extracts. Once used for an essay, they should be kept for possible future projects.

2. Loose-leaf ring binders containing notes on A4 sheets. Write on one side of the paper only on the A4 pads, double-spaced with margins to make any additions easier. You may need dividers to separate different aspects of a lengthy project.

3. 6" x 4" cards, easier to put in order by shuffling, particularly for an essay.

4. 5" x 3" bibliography cards; can be finally shuffled into alphabetical order.

5. 5" x 3" cards for jargon and formulae.

Note cards are illustrated on page 42.

CASE STUDIES

Neil joins a research team

The Sociology tutor had given the fifth year class a photocopy of an article by Seamus Milne in *The Guardian* of 7 September 1993, 'A movement born out of conflict', about the history of the Trades Union

Congress. He asked them what points in it would be relevant for an essay on the following topic:

'To what extent has the power of the trade unions decreased since 1980?' *GCSE Sociology, June 1993 (ULEAC).*

Neil, who always reads the last paragraph of anything first, declared that the relevant points were well summed up in the last paragraph and he read it, when asked to:

The TUC has had the industrial and political stuffing knocked out of it. It faces the twin threats of an ever tighter legal and industrial vice and increasingly assertive super-unions convinced they can get along fine without it. But anyone expecting an early demise of the old carthorse would be ill-advised to hold their breath. If the debates of 125 years ago are anything to go by, the TUC was born bemoaning its fate.

Tutor comment

A good start Neil, the tutor said. They would all do the essay, but first they would work together on creating a reading list and making notes. There were four groups and each member would have a specific task. The groups would go in shifts to the local library.

'Group 1 will look for information on how the law has changed since Mrs Thatcher's time. Group 2: how many unions are there now and what has happened to them since they were founded? Group 3: what has been the relationship between the TUC and the super-unions? Group 4 will bring the history up to date. Explain the union policies of the current General Secretary and Prime Minister, for example.

'Each group will divide into three pairs, one to list books and journalism, one to list organisations, and the third to do interviews. Note these suggestions, but of course add your own ideas.

'Books: try starting with an encyclopedia article to get an overall picture, and a book list, though it will be a bit out of date. Look through the library catalogue or database under TUC and related headings: the library assistants know you're coming and they're keen to help if you need it. Newspaper and magazine articles: try *The Times Index* and *British Humanities Index* which lists recent articles in various publications under headings. Also keep an eye open for any coverage in the papers from now on. Organisations: try the *Directory of British Associations*. Look for any organisation that might supply literature.

Check with me first and I'll select one or two and make the contacts for you. Interviews: come to me with some names and I'll make any necessary contacts.

'Some of you have been using the library but finding that you can waste a lot of time there unless you know exactly what you're looking for and where you'll find it. This time it should be different. If you were doing the essay all on your own, you would make yourself a timetable for the different activities and decide on the best order. I hope.'

Marjorie misreads another student's notes

'How effective are the media in their watchdog role?' is the topic being tackled by Marjorie in the A-Level Sociology class. She had got into a muddle. She had copied the notes of another student when she had missed a class and there were some notes she didn't understand.

Under the heading FOR was 'The media supplts ordy ppls rts' (Westergaard, 1977)' and under AGAINST was 'Media rarely ld in compn (Cirino, 1973)'. She went back to the supplier.

'The media supplements orderly people's riots?'

'Not exactly. That's an "r". The media supports ordinary people's rights.'

'Media rarely loud in competition?'

'No, media rarely lead in a campaign.'

They had a laugh, but Marjorie had to return for further translations. When she had added notes from the texts she had to go to her tutor. She had too many notes and didn't see how to put them in order.

Tutor comment

'This is quite a long project,' the tutor said, 'so it would be best to divide it up. Keep all notes on campaigns, for example, together, on one side of a page or pages. Or use cards. Then when you're ready to write, you can shuffle your notes in the order of your plan — or experiment with different orders.'

The tutor said that the notes she had copied, from the class she had missed, could be inserted into her notes from the texts.

Wide margins and double spacing should be left for this purpose. When there are a lot of lectures or tutorials, for example at university, he said that some students draw a line down the page and put lecture and text notes side by side.

'You've learnt that it can be unwise to borrow other students' lecture notes. Apart from the fact that you might misread the handwriting, notes reflect the state of knowledge of the student who makes them, not your own. Your friend knew quite a lot about newspaper campaigns so she merely made the references to the two books I mentioned. She put the authors in brackets fortunately to show the points were facts based on the expert authors' evidence — not quite the same as self-evident facts, such as the earth is round. If she, or you, had left them out you might have stated these points as if they were your own, or as if they needed no evidence.

'Notice you misread partly because your knowledge wasn't as great. Also you got a false impression perhaps that campaigns were not so important. You would have made different emphases if you'd been there. It's what's called the bias of a student's note-taking.'

'I think that I could do with more biases of that kind,' Marjorie said.

'Work in groups more, and share your ideas. You'll find other students with similar biases, so if you *have* to borrow notes you'll find some more use to you. Better still, work in small groups and pass your notes around the circle and then discuss them. I've been trying to get you to do that since the beginning of the year.'

'Sir, I know you're Welsh and you sing in a choir, but remember we're English and very reserved about such things. We tend to just work in pairs.'

Walter tries a for-and-against pattern

Walter Jeffrey was planning a short warm-up essay for his Foundation English Literature course. The title is:

> How far is it true to say that word-processors help you to write better?

His tutor has suggested in the instruction sheet sent that he would be dealing with informed opinions (including his own opinion based on his own experience) rather than self-evident facts or facts based on substantial evidence.

Walter decided he didn't have an opinion to start with. He would have to collect ideas and think about them. He began to make notes in two columns as follows as they came into his head, in the order shown:

AGAINST	FOR
(1) Just an instrument	(2) Can correct quickly and move blocks of text around
(3) Can make you *feel* it's better because mechanics are easier	(4) Programs to check spelling and even grammar

(5) Easier: can make you less fussy.

(6) Easier: you don't mind correcting many drafts.

At this stage Walter realised that the way he was thinking was a repetitive pattern of each point suggesting its opposite. He took another sheet of paper and began rewriting:

just an instrument

but corrects quickly

but only *feels* better bec easier

but more time for the writing

but can make you less fussy

In his introduction, he decided, he would probably have to explain that his approach to the title was: 'help' means 'make it easier' (to write better), but balanced against this was the fact of inherent laziness. Some writers would use the extra time and energy to make it better, others would reduce their efforts. But he wasn't sure yet. First he would continue with the thinking in 'buts'. Then he would take each aspect (mechanics, speed, and so on) and set advantages against disadvantages in the same way.

He could support arguments with the many technical facts he knew about word-processors, but he would need to weigh in with other highly informed opinion. He would send a questionnaire round his colleagues at work. For opinions without too much evidence behind them he would use words like 'may be' and 'theory', as his tutor suggested. How fortunate to start this English Literature course with an essay that was firmly rooted in the real world — and *his* world at that!

SUMMARY

The main research skills are:

- relating the research to the topic at all stages of the work
- knowing how to use a library, to observe and interview
- reading purposefully (using the formula SQ3R)
- note-taking and organising notes effectively.

4

Putting Your Ideas into Shape

'Thinking means connecting things, and stops if they cannot be connected.' G K Chesterton, *Orthodoxy*.

EFFECTIVE THINKING

For essays, thinking means **connecting the knowledge** you have amassed about the subject, shaped and adapted by your own thoughts and ideas, to the demands of the topic. Planning means making your thinking effective: putting what you have to say in logical order, with clear connections between the parts so that you achieve unity and coherence. In practice, you are thinking and planning simultaneously, but giving extra attention to the more creative approach — finding ideas — or to the more analytical approach — putting the ideas in order, when required. Try out the various suggestions in this chapter and discover what kind of switching back and forward between the two suits you best.

What are the hardest things about essay planning?

Thinking effectively is particularly difficult at certain points in the essay planning process. At which point do you find it hardest? Consider these emergency points:

1. At the start: when first confronted with the topic.

2. When switching gear, *eg:* from gathering information to imposing order on it.

3. When the plan doesn't work — some connections are weak or lacking.

4. When you have digressed.

5. When a clear conclusion is slow to emerge.

6. When an introduction is elusive.

7. When blocked at any point in thinking, planning or writing.

(Emergency points in the course of writing are dealt with in later chapters.)

PLANNING TACTICS

The aim of this chapter is to describe various planning tactics that will help you to surmount barriers to effective thinking. Some or all might be employed for one essay. Any of them might help at one of the emergency points. The tactics are:

●   Building on your controlling idea.

●   Brainstorming for ideas: the creative approach.

●   Putting your points in order: the analytical approach.

●   Finding the best pattern to develop.

●   Choosing the plan that fits the topic.

●   Vetting your plan.

BUILDING ON YOUR CONTROLLING IDEA

Your controlling idea is a summary of what you have to say in your essay in one sentence. You need a controlling idea round which the parts will gather to give your essay unity and coherence before you attempt a final plan. You can call that controlling idea a thesis, a theme, an explanation, a considered view — depending on the kind of essay.

You may have found a good controlling idea before making notes. It may have been immediately suggested by the essay title. Topics requiring your views on capital punishment (controlling idea: it should be/not be restored), or the significance of Brutus's role in *Julius Caesar* may well have been anticipated. You may well have a thesis already prepared, and at the end of note-taking it may not have changed.

On the other hand, your ideas might come thick and fast; and at the end of note-taking you may still be far from deciding on a controlling idea. You still don't know what you think, or you still don't see how to argue a particular case or explain some process. If so, don't plan too soon.

Write first, plan later

Don't worry about it. Tell yourself it's because you're creative. Write first, plan later. Read through your notes but don't be daunted if they are numerous. Either you eat your notes, or they eat you. Put them aside.

Make false starts, tear up and start again. A plan, together with a controlling idea, will emerge. You can then go back to the notes to flesh it out.

For the more intractable subjects — a Moral Philosophy topic such as 'Is happiness the thing to aim at?' — you may find it more productive to keep up a flow of several drafts, reshaping and refining your ideas as you go.

You may prefer to write first, plan later, or keep drafting, whatever the topic.

BRAINSTORMING FOR IDEAS

This is particularly useful at the start of thinking, or of planning, or at the start of writing, or at any point where you get stuck or find your ideas too predictable. The techniques liberate the imagination, and produce fresh ideas. They can evoke patterns that will show you how to order your facts and ideas in interesting ways, whether you're working from notes or not.

- **Brainstorming** means experimenting with word and idea associations, particularly making unusual associations, to see what happens.

Before giving examples of this technique, let's put ourselves in a situation that will benefit from it. Suppose you are faced with a general (or 'creative') GCSE essay of 500 words assigned without warning, to be done quickly or even under exam conditions.

Example

Let's take, for example: 'Have the feminists gone too far?' If you are returning to GCSE from the 'Land of the Seriously Adult', you may well have much to say about the subject. You may see immediately how you would analyse it, and argue it (especially if your partner has just left you).

If, however, you are 15 you may find polemical topics like this quite daunting. You have not yet gathered enough knowledge of life to have any strong views on the subject or to have read others' views or to see how to break it up.

Your immediate reaction might be 'Dunno'. Don't worry. The tutor is not expecting wisdom nor even balanced argument in these circumstances. What is hoped for is a **point of view expressed persuasively** (good practice towards balanced argument). It can be entertaining, even humorous.

When you have paraphrased it ('To what extent do you think that the campaigners for recognising the rights and increasing the opportunities of women have produced harm as well as benefits?') you may find ideas beginning to arrive. But you can build further, with 'associations'.

Using the five Ws association

Now for the associations. Associate your essay subject with words that relate to real life. An essay must provide evidence for points made. Evidence means examples. Examples can be found or created by associating your subject with:

people	(who)
places	(where)
activities, events, situations	(what)
times	(when)
reasons	(why)

To this add processes (how). In brackets are the 'five W questions plus How' that the newspaper reporter keeps in mind to collect information for a report.

You might find these questions easier to use. How do they relate to your topic? You are now ready to write down how the evidence might be grouped:

Who	working class people, middle-class, housewives, people in different occupations/professions...
Where	at school, at home, at work, at leisure...
What	housework, family life, education, occupations ...

When	times/occasions when feminist campaigners have delayed progress
Why	arguments such as 'it's a man's world' or 'women deny their nature trying to be men' to explain why particular views of feminism are held
How	ways in which women/men are discriminated against.

Using people and perspectives

A slimline version of the above technique can be described as People and Perspectives. For example, you are faced with:

What was Oliver Cromwell's quarrel with King Charles I?

Your interest has been firmly engaged in British History but you can't see a path through all the facts (or you're sitting an exam and feel hopeless at remembering facts). Furthermore, we'll say, you're young, and like most young students you tend to repeat the generalisations of your history texts without fully grasping them.

Example 1
People and Perspectives means how do (or would) certain people, or groups of people, or professions, or institutions, react to (or within) your subject? Let's apply it to the history topic. You've already got the people, Oliver and Charles. So the approach is: how did they react to each other? What was Cromwell's perspective on the quarrel? — rather than: what were the details of the constitutional argument? To do this, imagine yourself as Oliver Cromwell: what is your *attitude* to King Charles and the way he rules? By moving back from the clouds of facts you are freer to think and to reveal your historical imagination, which a tutor bombarded with undigested facts may be grateful for. The significant facts you need for signposts are also more likely to present themselves when you are thinking in a fruitful way.

Example 2
Applying People and Perspectives to the feminism topic, how do certain key groups of people (professions, for example) relate to feminism? How far have opportunities for women advanced within them? The Anglican Church immediately comes to mind. Teachers? Lawyers? Doctors? Actors?

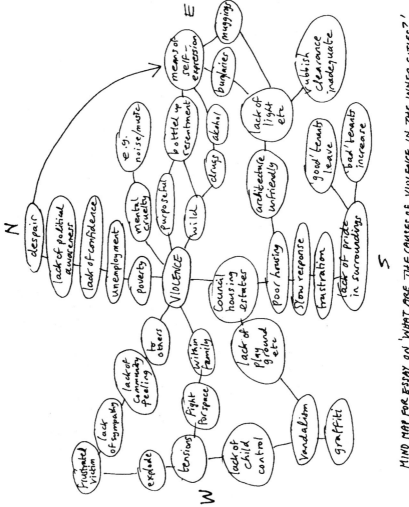

MIND MAP FOR ESSAY ON 'WHAT ARE THE CAUSES OF VIOLENCE IN THE INNER CITIES?'

Should there be more prisons or fewer?

will benefit — if it is not too obvious — from showing perspectives of ex-prisoners, social workers, police, victims of crime and priests as well as from (if it is sociology) the theories of the academics.

Using random associations

Brainstorming more freely may be worth trying if nothing of much interest or originality is emerging from your thinking and planning.

- **Random association** means putting alongside a concept — let's say 'punishment' — words picked out at random from a dictionary.

Here we go. Punishment and — dedication — euphemism — H-bomb — orphanage — sellotape — squid — triangle — woman. Punishment and euphemism might be an interesting connection. H-bomb and orphanage also suggests a train of thought.

Bringing humour into your thinking is one more way of escaping from the straitjacket of logic that can prevent you from seeing things in an original way. Edward de Bono's books on 'lateral thinking' describe many more liberating techniques.

Using mind maps

Write down your word and idea associations in a pattern called a mind map (also known as a mind web, a 'spider' or a concept tree). You can develop the map into a logical plan if it needs more order, or work on it until it makes a comprehensive plan in itself. The mind map is particularly useful as a visual plan for an essay exam. It is also worth trying for note-taking, whether for essays or business reports.

On page 54 is a mind map for an essay on 'What are the causes of violence in inner cities?'

Setting out points one by one under the headings in the formal manner might be a safer way of being comprehensive. But the mind map makes you think of (and see at a glance when you've finished) the more surprising relationships, like seeing a landscape from the air.

Memory check

Close the book, and in 60 words (20 for each) write explanations of the three brainstorming techniques — 5 Ws, People and Perspectives, and random associations (if preferred do it orally with a fellow-student as monitor). Finally, compare with the text on pages 52–53 and 55.

PUTTING YOUR POINTS IN ORDER

When imposing order on given facts and opinions, rather than dis-covering ideas, is likely to be the emphasis, you will benefit most from formal plans. Base them on:

Introduction	beginning
Body	middle
Conclusion	end

Your planned introduction and conclusion may be provisional until you have finished writing. On the other hand, if you *have* come to a definite conclusion at the planning stage, or at the start of writing, it will help you to avoid digressing.

FINDING THE BEST PATTERN TO DEVELOP

From your quick read-through of the notes or from the rough sketch of your ideas, as described above, let a pattern or patterns emerge:

● Is it a narrative, requiring mainly a chronological order?

● Does the narrative need further ordering — some kind of historical exposition for example — origins, developments, effects?

● Will further subdivision be necessary: for example, political, social, economic?

● Should there be a climax or anti-climax order — most important first or most important last?

● Is it an exposition/argument requiring an order of cause and effect?

● Will an exposition be done by definition, analysis, clarification (notably by clearing away misconceptions about the subject), com-parison, explanation of relationships?

● Will an argument be developed by presentation of evidence, by analogy, by induction (from the particular to the general), by deduc-tion (from the general to the particular), or from past experience (for example, you can expect certain trends in the economy because it is cyclical)?

The more essays you write, the more instinctively you will choose the right shape for the purpose. Here are some techniques of the formal kind.

CHOOSING A PLAN TO FIT THE TOPIC

Building points into paragraphs

A straightforward essay needing little exposition or argument can be planned with a list of points. Five hundred words on:

A child's visit to the British Museum

for example, might be ordered under:

1. Mummies.

2. Weapons.

3. Gold.

4. Jewellery.

5. Sculpture.

6. The Magna Carta.

Now you can give a paragraph to each point; 70 words for each paragraph (total 420 words) would leave you, say, 50 words for an introductory and 30 words for a concluding paragraph. 'What happens when you are arrested' and 'How to cook a beef stew' would be equally easy to arrange.

Question-per-paragraph plan

The questions that it was suggested could be raised before, during and after planning could be put in order and used as a question-per-paragraph plan. Let's see how that would work with

Should parents be responsible for the crimes of their children?

Your questions might run something like this:

- Is the quality of parental guidance deteriorating?

- Is there insufficient discipline/motivation to learn in the schools?

- Are the resources of the police insufficient to cope with delinquents?

- Is the law inadequate and are the courts too busy to cope?

- Do the media (and particularly TV) set up too many unworthy role models?

- Do current standards of behaviour in society at large provide bad examples?

At 500 words it would be an opinion piece. If you had 1000 words, you would no doubt be expected to do some research. Your questions would be added to and improved. You might then give more than one paragraph to any issue that demanded more space.

Statement-per-paragraph plan
This is particularly suitable for a straight-through logical exposition/ argument, and if you insert the links the writing-up will stay on the rails. For example, an Economics essay on **'The Costly Misconceptions about Risks'** might be planned like this (links in *italic*):

1. *Introduction.* Examples of misconception: the car driver is 18 times more likely to die in a car crash than a train passenger (recent Royal Society report).

2. *Yet* continual safety improvements to trains paid for by increases in fares.

3. *This results* in more people taking to roads — which are more dangerous.

4. *These decisions* are based on many public misconceptions about daily risks (reference to Royal Society report and article in Economics journal):

   (a) Building regulations: the estimated cost is £23 million for each life saved

   (b) Cancers are considered twice as frequent as heart diseases (but the reverse is true)

   (c) Murders are considered to be as common as strokes (but strokes are ten times more frequent).

5.   Conclusion: The blame for getting *expenditure decisions* wrong can be attributed to public mistrust of experts (however justified sometimes).

Producing a detailed outline

When you have a lot of notes the formal plan will force you to work out how your points should be connected. It will remind you to make links where the connections are not obvious, and provide the framework on which to peg all your references, interviews, quotes, quotations, anecdotes and examples.

It's a good idea to note points for your introduction and conclusion. A fairly detailed schematic outline for an essay, with some linking indicated, and a plan for a business report, with comments on their similarities, are given in Appendices C and D.

VETTING YOUR PLAN

Here is a checklist for vetting your plan:

●   Is there a unified theme with a logical progression?

●   Is every point necessary?

●   Are they well connected?

●   Does the introduction make it clear what the essay is all about, and what the viewpoint is?

●   Do introduction and conclusion chime?

●   Is the conclusion firmly backed up by the evidence of the body?

TASK

(Study: 5 minutes. Writing the plan: 20 minutes)
First study the detailed outline for an essay in Appendix C. Then make a detailed outline of the same length for an essay on:

> Has the anti-smoking campaign gone too far?

Include brief Introduction and Conclusion sections as in the model. Come to a conclusion for or against, but put both sides of the argument. Use the following points, which are out of order, for the body, and add to them:

1. Danger to health of others.

2. Government gains much revenue from sales of tobacco.

3. Anti-social behaviour: 'dirty habit', smell on clothes, breath, *etc.*

4. 'An addiction rather than a pleasure.'

5. Bad example to children.

6. Dangers to health: cancer, emphysema, *etc.*

7. Smoking is a basic human right.

8. 'A pleasure rather than an addiction.'

9. The cost to the taxpayer of keeping smokers alive/in health.

CASE STUDIES

Christine adds facts to personal experience

Christine thought she knew all she needed to know about home deliveries of newspapers because it had been her source of pocketmoney for two years. Now there was a project for her group in the Business Studies class entitled:

> Are newsboys and newsgirls an endangered species?

and she realised that there was a great deal she had to learn. She asked questions of the newsagent she worked for and found that it was a sore point with him.

'Another example of EU stupidity,' he said. 'They want to stop children under 15 from doing anything but "light work". They're working on new regulations that might make it impossible for us to use children for this job.'

From Christine's group's questions the following were selected:

- How many children in the UK do regular home deliveries of newspapers?

- How easy are they to find?

- Are they satisfied with their wages?

- What are the dangers of the job (apart from back breaking)?

- What exactly are the regulations that the EU might bring in?

- Would UK children have to come under the new EU rules?

- What other means of distribution are being considered in this country to replace children?

Tutor comment
'You did quite well,' the tutor said. 'Here's some information that will answer most of those questions so that you can start planning your project. For homework, find the answer to that last question. Go to the library. Find out about the Newspaper Publishing Association and the Newsagents' Association, or whatever it's called. See if you can shed any light on the question. But don't start phoning them up!'

David's need to focus clearly

David was given some advice by his A-Level Law class tutor on how to improve a first draft of:

> How do the courts distinguish between offer and
> invitation to treat?

Tutor comment
'Don't forget to underline the cases to indicate how the courts deal with this issue. The examiner wants to be able to look quickly through your essay to see if you have covered the relevant ground.

'Now look at your first paragraph. You give a clear definition of an offer. Second paragraph: you cite a case, at reasonable length, which implies a differentiation between offers and invitations to treat — let's call them ITTs — but you haven't mentioned ITTs yet, never mind defined them.

'Your third paragraph does that, and then brings in a series of cases turning on the differentiation. You say, "It has been held that goods displayed in a shop, or in a catalogue, or at an auction are not offered so that a buyer can insist on a purchase. The display is an invitation to treat, the offer is made by the buyer tendering the money or making a bid which may then be accepted by the seller . . ." Fine, and it gets better, though the next, complex case cited should have focused more clearly on the issue. There's irrelevant detail. Every word must be relevant in Law essays. Note in your first paragraph the issue or issues raised by the question. You should have defined both terms immediately. Make your conclusion a direct answer to the question, summing up the evidence you've supplied.'

'What was it you said last week sir? "Don't be clever, be relevant". I'm trying to keep that in mind.'

Ann needs help from her friends

Ann was collecting her thoughts for a British History essay on:

How racist are the professions?

She had written one paragraph to see how she could get into the subject. She was reading this out to two of her black friends.

' "Black children end up in slum schools. At the other end they're woefully under-represented in the professions. Not surprising, is it? The trouble is that they're being fragmented. It would be better with the old black consciousness. It would pull them together in unity and give them more power. There are too many divisions. Muslim schools for instance . . ." '

'What?' asked the Muslim friend.

'Let that go for a moment. Carry on Ann.'

' "At the same time there's upward mobility going on among the blacks, and they're getting to the universities. . ." '

'Hullo.'

' "But at the other end of their education . . ." '

'You've said that.'

' "At the other end there's only a trickle into the top professions. Why?" That's where I've got so far. I think I'll give examples from a few professions, and a commentary after each example. The solicitor who is reluctant to work with a black barrister — of course he says it's the client who doesn't like it.'

'You will have to have a case study rather than anecdotes though, I think.'

'Which professions?' Ann was then asked.

'The three worst.'

'No. Better would be the best and the worst, and one in between.'

'Give me more questions.'

'How many blacks get to the top ranks of the professions?'

'Are they encouraged at school to go for these professions?'

'What are the recruitment policies in the different professions?'

'Is promotion a lot slower for blacks?'

'I could take these aspects through each of the professions, couldn't I?

'Well, you can start with a middle of the road case, to lift off. Give an idea of the whole career, from recruitment onwards.'

'I might find one in *The Guardian*. Where would I be without my black friends?'

'That would be a good note to end on.'

SUMMARY

Planning is a way of making sure you think effectively, so that your essay has unity and coherence, with all the connections in the right places. Plans are of two kinds: 'creative' or 'informal' and 'linear-logical', or 'formal.'

Creative plans are produced by such brainstorming experiments as The Five Ws association — asking five W questions plus How. This can be simplified into the People and Perspectives formula. The game of Random Associations is another technique.

5

Making Your Essay Coherent

Carry the reader with you by keeping to the point and making clear connections.

You may find it easier to write your essay if you get the introduction right first – you then see how to proceed. Or you may prefer to get the conclusion right first – seeing the destination all the time keeps you on track.

But spending time on these parts is usually more fruitful when you see what you've said, when you've built the body. Building the body, therefore, is what the next two chapters will concentrate on.

THE THREE-PART STRUCTURE

Since unity and coherence are the subject of this chapter, let's summarise how the three parts hang together:

Introduction

Indicate:

* what you understand by the title

* what your objectives are

* which aspects of the subject you will deal with

* what you will explain or argue.

The body

* Build up your explanation/argument with ideas, opinions and facts.

- Support key points by examples and other evidence, using your own thoughts and experience, and the statements of authorities.

Conclusion

- Sum up; return to the title, or echo it in some way.

- Show that you have answered the question, or arrived at a point of view; possibly speculating on the future.

This chapter will assume that you have collected the notes you need and are on the point of writing. This was identified as a possible emergency point in Chapter 4. It may be that you overdid the research and are deep in a forest of information with no pathway to be seen. Or you may have done not quite enough reading – there are gaps, and (to make it worse), you may not be sure exactly where they are. This chapter will show you how to:

- get in the mood to write
- start writing
- keep to the point.

GETTING IN THE MOOD TO WRITE

Essays can be competent but cold. You may have conceived yours with feeling. You may have fought hard to get it right, painstakingly searched for the right phrases, tinkered with the shape, only to find that the heat has dispersed, that the life and the soul have gone out of it.

With a deadline, you may not have time to *wait* for the mood to rewrite. In any case, this may be the worst thing you could do. Instead, you can **create the mood**.

When you start to write, make sure that you are full of interest in your subject, keen to communicate what you have to say. Much reading and thinking may have had a mind-numbing effect.

Getting warmed up

Here are three suggestions for loosening up and warming up (use one or more):

1. Talk to fellow students until your feeling re-emerges.

2. Skim through your notes to find a point, an argument, a telling image that excites you and gives you a starting point.

3. Read something near in subject-matter to your projected essay, but not too close — an article, perhaps, or a chapter of a book. Alternatively, a play, a film, or a TV programme may do the rekindling.

4. Your brain may need more oxygen. If so, going for a walk or a swim will help.

These tactics can be tried out at any stage of writer's block.

STARTING TO WRITE

Here are six ways of starting to write. Use the combination that suits you.

- Talk yourself into it.

- Take a starting point, and plunge in.

- Re-start from warm.

- Correct as you go.

- Extend paragraph to essay.

- Use a mind map.

Talk yourself into it

Select your audience, tell them (briefly) what you've found out about the subject, and see how they react. Do they understand what you're saying, or are you still far from getting your thoughts in order? The conversation will force you to get your thoughts in better order, and a controlling idea for your essay might emerge, if it hasn't already.

Ask them:

'What would *you* want to know from this essay?'
'What questions would *you* ask if you were doing it?
'What would be *your* key question?'

You might get a provisional introduction out of them that will send you on your way. Something like:

'Mention capital punishment in the course of conversation and you may be bombarded with the following points of view. . .' Or: '. . . and you may find that what you thought were your firm convictions quickly begin to waver. . .' Or: 'Whatever views people hold on capital punishment, very few would disagree that. . .'

Take a starting point, and plunge in

It might be an anecdote, a joke, an image, a quote, a question. If its relevance hits you between the eyes, put it down, and keep writing. You have thrown a stone into a lake and you're watching the patterns made by the ripples.

You might decide to omit the first paragraph or two when you've come to the end, but it will have served its purpose.

Keep going. You don't have to be linear. Learn from the painter and the sculptor. Jump into the middle and build round it. A portrait painter won't labour for hours getting every detail of the eyes right before moving down. If you come to a gap, and your notes don't seem to help, put 'gap' (with any ideas about further reading), and carry on.

Re-start from warm

When the writing takes several sessions, especially when there are days in between, make sure you don't have to re-start from cold. Get into the next sentence or two of your essay, knowing how you will continue. If necessary, leave yourself a note or two (along the lines of 'Don't forget the milk') as well, indicating what to do next.

Correct as you go

Are you a corrector-as-you-go? That way may work better for you than concentrating on maintaining the flow of a draft, especially if you have a word processor. You may go through several drafting journeys in one continuous operation. But you could consider that certain essays which tend to be produced by going deeper into layers of thought, one after the other (philosophy, history, political theory) might suffer from being beaten up before they're strong enough to fight back.

A compromise is usually best. Find better words and phrases as you go, but avoid making radical changes. Print out drafts and make major alterations on these. Keep previous drafts until you're sure of the end product. When a machine makes it so easy to delete and rearrange your sentences, at least give them some time to speak up for themselves.

We shall now see how to adapt brainstorming techniques for planning into techniques to get you writing. But first:

Memory check

Write one sentence on each:

1. What is the 'people and perspectives' formula?

2. Explain the question-per-paragraph plan.

3. Explain the statement-per-paragraph plan.

Compare what you have written with what is said about these matters on pages 53 and 57–59.

Now here is a strategy for rapidly turning this kind of planning into a draft.

Extend paragraph to essay

Take, for example the topic:

> Should parents be responsible for the crimes of their children?

Run the questions listed on pages 58 on into the form of a paragraph. Call this your original, or **summary-foundation** paragraph.

Reorder the questions more effectively, if you see a way. Replace any of the questions, if better ones occur to you. The advantage of putting them all into one paragraph first is that you begin to see them, not as separate points, but as points that together make a whole. The unity of that original paragraph will be reflected in your finished essay.

Now, in this original paragraph, after each question you could put a statement — a rough guide to the kind of answer you might develop — or another question. Underline a link or two if they come to mind, or wait until they come to mind in the course of writing up.

Example
You might begin:

> Is the quality of parental guidance deteriorating? There seems little doubt that a general weakening of religious and moral convictions makes parents less confident about guiding their offspring. Is there *a similar cause* for the lack of discipline and of motivation to learn reported in many schools . . .?

You could then use your notes for these additional statements or questions, or you could develop your thoughts as you go.

You are now ready to begin the essay proper. Each pair of sentences (question plus statement or two questions) makes the beginning of each paragraph of your essay. Fill out each paragraph as you go. Swoop into your notes when you feel the need, but if you have a lot of notes avoid slowing yourself down into a writer's block. The whole point of this strategy is to get your writing flowing without delay. The original paragraph might be adapted for an Introduction.

Use a mind map

Let us see how the mind map on page 54 could quickly get you writing. After studying this for a minute or so, you could number and label five sectors:

What are the causes of violence in inner cities?

1. Violence defined — kinds of violence and where directed (items close to the centre).

2. Various general causes (North).

3. How tensions build up — explode — children learn violent ways (South West).

4. Crimes of violence — how they follow attempts to escape from causes/effects of poverty (alcohol, drugs) (East).

5. Violence breeding violence — for example, in the worst housing estates (South).

You could then decide on an order: let's say as it is, 1 to 5. Then try a (provisional) introduction, perhaps like this:

Violence breeds violence. There is the violence done to people's self-esteem by unemployment, poverty and growing despair. That can destroy initiative and turn into a consuming guilt. There is the violence bred of frustration inside the family or immediate community as people fight for space and dignity. It can explode out of despair, controlled and uncontrolled, It can escape, via alcohol and drugs, into crime. Causes are hard to distinguish from effects. In the worst of the

Extract from art history essay showing connectives

The world of art is shadowy, especially where it meets the world of money. It is not easy to see things clearly, to get all the information you need. When hundreds of thousands of pounds are involved, conversation tends to become more and more tight-lipped. Apart from that, especially with old masters, it isn't always clear what is a forgery and what is not. Van Dyck, Rembrandt and Corot are only the most notorious examples of great painters who signed paintings on which their students did most of the work.

The important sale-rooms such as Christie's and Sotheby's rigorously check attributions, and there are established formulae for indicating the degree of doubt. Giving the artist's name in full, including christian name, means that the sale-room believes it is the artist's work; giving the initials only of christian names means: possibly by the artist, certainly the same school; giving the surname only suggests that the work is an imitation of the master. When many lots have to be sold rapidly, however, there are likely to be one or two fakes, as well as a fair number of mistaken attributions. In country auction rooms the uncertainties in the attributing may be greater.

When it comes to known (proven) forgeries, there are different attitudes in different countries. In some countries they are destroyed; in others, such as France, they are locked up. In the UK they may remain in circulation: it is a question of 'caveat emptor' — buyer beware — when you buy from a sale-room which turns out to be mistaken about an attribution made in good faith.

rundown inner city housing estates the causes and effects of violence are in a vicious spiral.

You might even decide that your provisional introduction wasn't necessary at all, that it had served its purpose as a way of warming up, and that the paragraph or two that followed was effectively the introduction. Or you might decide to rewrite it completely, now that your thoughts are in better order.

KEEPING TO THE POINT

An essay must keep to the point. Be as simple and direct as the subject and the purpose allow. Your essay must have unity and coherence. The parts should be in orderly, logical sequence adding up to one theme, and they should be clearly linked. To repeat: keep the title in front of you as you write.

Try to carry the reader along in the flow, as the experienced driver carries a passenger in a car. Confident in your ability, the reader should see clearly where the vehicle is going. A different destination may have been preferred, but there should be no complaints about the route to the destination that was chosen.

Using a network of connectives

The main techniques that achieve unity and coherence involve using **connectives**. Study the extract from an art history essay on page 70. It is entitled:

Explain the attitudes to art forgeries in the UK and show how these attitudes are reflected in the way the forgeries are dealt with.

Notes

The most important *key terms*, related to forgery, are boxed.

Repetitions: 'world', 'what is . . . what is not', 'artists', 'work', 'giving', 'different attitudes . . . different countries'

Echoes: 'money . . . pounds', 'great painters' . . . 'artists' . . . 'master', 'sale-rooms . . . auction rooms'

Miscellaneous links:. 'Apart from that', 'only', 'however', 'When it comes to. . .'

The network of lines indicates how the key concept is repeated through synonyms and near-synonyms. They make a web that holds the discussion together. Other connectives that contribute to the meshing are also shown.

Don't fake connections that your essay lacks. If there is a gap in the weave of your essay, dropping a connective in won't fill it. Purpose, content, clear understanding of the subject, and overall structure, therefore, come first: the connectives will be dictated by these factors. It is best if they come naturally out of your thinking, whether (as we have seen) in the course of planning, or in the course of writing.

Since the way your thoughts are connected is clearer to you than to your reader, you are more likely to have too few connectives than too many in a first draft. Scrutinise the draft to identify where clearer connectives are needed. When you say, 'This leads us to . . .' is it clear where you've been? Take special care at the beginnings of paragraphs, where you are changing gear.

Types of connectives to use

Key words and ideas repeated
These will include the echoes of synonyms and near-synonyms. In the paragraph-essay on violence there are:

violence	escape
destroy	crime
consuming	vicious
fight	spiral
explode	

In the art history extract are:

shadowy	mistaken attributions
forgery	uncertainties
doubt	forgeries
possibly	they
imitation	mistaken
fakes	

Pronouns, demonstratives, definite article and comparative words

These refer to statements already made. Examples are: he, she, it, we, this, that, these, those, the, equal, similar, such, bigger, the former, the latter.

Repeated grammatical patterns

Violence: 'There is the violence . . . there is the violence . . ., it can . . . it can . . .' (Use in moderation).

Art history: 'In some countries . . . in others . . . in the UK'.

Signposting

You say, in effect, the foregoing has covered *that*; what follows will cover *this*. For example: '*Not only* do visitors find the towns more lively than they had imagined, *but* the climate is also a pleasant surprise.' Do it subtly, though.

Miscellaneous links

Addition:	and, furthermore, moreover, what is more.
Contrast:	but, however, nevertheless, on the other hand, if the truth be told, admittedly, granted, it's true that.
Consequence:	so. therefore, the result was that . . . hence, consequently, as a result . . .
Example:	for example, for instance, to put this more clearly.

Don't over-use these common links, however, just because they are readily available. The weather forecasters have constantly to guard against their 'buts'. Otherwise you will hear: 'It is a sunshine and showers day. This morning it will be mainly sunny, dry periods with some cloud . . . But showers will spread . . . But by late evening . . .'

Use the longer linking phrases sometimes when you are changing gear. This will prepare the reader smoothly and give breathing space: the reader uses the space to let the thoughts you've aroused so far settle into the necessary pattern. Use the rather more unusual links if they fit: 'Whether this way of putting it is wholly acceptable is a matter for debate . . .' is the sort of thing. Take them out of the second draft if they sound garrulous.

TASK (15 minutes)

Here is a paragraph of a GCSE project on smoking based on a questionnaire. Rewrite, improving the order and the links, and more concisely. Reduce by about a half. Include only the points made.

Project on Smoking

I discovered that reasons for smoking include social reasons and others such as people enjoy it or the pressure from their work and other stresses. Another reason given is pure habit, for example after each meal, any time they have to wait for something, or have a difficult job to do or after doing a difficult job, to relax. Other people say it stimulates them or makes them feel more cheerful in themselves. The social reasons are, when people smoke they do it in front of their friends who also smoke, this is socialising. Not surprisingly, smoking at the pub with friends who also smoke was the most popular reason. If you go back a hundred years a survey would have shown socialising as the most important reason for smoking, because it was in the fashion. But nowadays the attitudes have changed, now it is drinking, while smoking is now a pest to society and people consider it as being anti-social. When people say they enjoy it I cannot comment because I am a non-smoker, but many people, when they try their first cigarette say 'Horrible!'

CASE STUDIES

Neil's argument lacks supporting evidence
Neil is an Arsenal fan, who watches most of their games, both home and away. He goes along with a group. They stand on the terraces wherever they still exist because that's where the atmosphere is. He is against all-seater grounds and said so in an essay titled 'Should Football Stadia be All-Seater?'

He made the following points in his first paragraph: the Hillsborough disaster, when many Liverpool football fans were killed after a barrier collapsed in front of a terrace, was not a good argument for all-seaters. The fencing was unsafe, and it was the fault of the police for not controlling the crowd.

He then wrote two paragraphs describing the poor facilities and lack of hygiene at certain clubs' grounds which he had visited: those at the all-seater grounds were no better than those at the grounds which were not all-seater. He ended the essay by saying that the all-seater grounds he had visited had been lacking in atmosphere, and this was the main reason he was against extending seating to existing grounds and building new all-seater grounds. Furthermore, all his friends were of the same opinion.

Tutor comment
'Some of the points you make would have been valid if you could have shown that they amounted to evidence — in other words, if you have collected figures that gave a much better idea of fans' views than "all my friends", and figures backing up some kind of economic argument. You have made up your mind and simply grabbed whatever points seem to back up your opinion. That is called "begging the question".

'Not only the terraces at the Hillsborough ground but those in other grounds in the country were found to be unsafe. The police may have been at fault, but that doesn't mean that there were not other problems. The argument about facilities is totally unconvincing. You say nothing about the arguments of those who are in favour of all-seating, not to mention the long report that supported all-seater stadiums.'

Marjorie lacks sympathy for fictional characters
Having mulled over her notes, Marjorie feels no desire to get more closely acquainted with the essay topic. She arranges to talk to her tutor.

Marjorie: I've got summaries of all the stories, and notes on themes and characters, but . . . 'Do Susan Hill's characters bring unhappiness on themselves or are they depicted as victims of external forces?' is what I call a soppy question.

Tutor: Literary questions do sometimes appear soppy at first sight.

Marjorie: Are we really supposed to *care* about these people?

Tutor: Sympathise perhaps. D H Lawrence said that the novel can lead our sympathies towards what is alive and away from things that are dead. Well, Susan Hill does that. Makes us sympathise without giving us a message or telling us what to think about them. She wants us to understand them and how life treats them. That's why the question is possible. It's for and against, and it's the quality of your argument and your sympathy that counts.

Marjorie: I am *interested* in them of course, as a psychiatrist would be. It's just that when I'm faced with such a question I tend to get irritated with them rather than sympathise. But I like what Lawrence said. I realise it's my fault.

Tutor: I think you will be able to sympathise with a wider range of characters in time. Don't force it. You can't force sympathies. Try to get interested in fictional characters and what happens to them. Whoever they are. Read good fiction and it will *lead* you, as Lawrence said.

Walter wavers between facts and opinions

Half way through an essay on Modern World History, Walter was glad of the opportunity to visit his tutor at the university. He put a pile of notes under the tutor's nose together with one of the books he had been taking notes from.

'You explained to me all about what's a fact and what's an opinion after my last essay, but I'm not sure what I've got here. You see, on page 42, about these letters the minister had been writing. He said to all his friends that he was sorry that because of drinking and gambling he had neglected his duties. Do I regard that as a fact or an opinion?'

The tutor rifled through the notes and a page or two of the book. 'The author says that the minister was accused of neglecting his duties and that there are 39 letters over a period of 18 months to his closest friends and colleagues referring to his deep regret about neglecting his duties.'

'But the minister was depressed,' said Walter. 'He may have exaggerated his guilt. I'm not sure at all that I should regard the neglect as a fact or an opinion.'

'Take the author's word for it as a fact, since he takes it as a fact, that the minister neglected his duties. His evidence is a lot of letters. There are one or two other pieces of evidence here. Much more than just an opinion or an informed guess. And this author is a renowned authority. Put in brackets after your note author and page number in case you want to check back on it. If you found some other reference casting doubt on it then you would check again and balance the two pieces of evidence against each other. Then you might put your own opinion in square brackets to suggest how you might develop the subject.'

'When it comes to politics, I'm full of square brackets,' said Walter mournfully.

SUMMARY

Getting started

1. *In the mood* for writing means feeling keen to communicate, your ideas ready to flow. Talking, reading, exposing yourself to the

subject, or exercise may help to get you in the mood.

2. *Starting and re-starting* an essay can also be helped on by conversation. If an obviously suitable start doesn't quickly present itself, choose any possible way in: an image or a quote, for example.

3. *Once the essay is launched*, its momentum can be kept up by various strategies. Choose the strategy that suits the kind of essay, and your temperament. You may prefer to correct as you go, or to maintain the flow by completing drafts before correcting.

4. *Brainstorming techniques* for getting started include extending summary-paragraph to essay, and using a mind map.

Keeping to the point

1. Keeping to the point means being as *simple and direct* as possible, with one controlling idea and with parts logically connected.

2. *Connectives* must be used skilfully so that you ensure clarity and coherence.

3. A *well-structured essay* is achieved by language skills, but it may lack life unless your *interest* in the subject has been so awakened that you have a strong desire to communicate it.

6

Giving Your Work Conviction

'True ease in writing comes from art, not chance.
As those move easiest who have learned to dance'

Alexander Pope (1688–1744)

This chapter will describe some effective ways to:

- **narrate** a story or piece of history

- **describe** a scene or a process

- **analyse and explain** a situation, process or procedure

- **argue** a case and present it persuasively

- **fit a pattern** to your subject

- **slot in your evidence**

- **use anecdotes, quotes and quotations**.

Each skill demands its own patterns. A combination of two or more patterns is usually required in an essay. **Argument** has to follow some analysis of the topic — division into its different aspects — and some **exposition** — explanation of the ways different viewpoints are arrived at. **Analysis** often follows description, particularly the special kind of description that is the defining of key terms. **Narration** — putting facts and events in an appropriate order — is rarely separate from description or from exposition. History is 'expository narration'. For convenience we shall discuss each skill separately.

HOW TO NARRATE

The narrative patterns in essays (following such instructional terms as 'relate', 'state' and 'trace') are clear and straightforward; they are not slowed down by unnecessary description. Chronological patterns are common but may be cut across by exposition patterns. For example, the extent of damage done by riots (**effects**) may need to be dealt with before **causes**.

A clear path to a climax

Climax order is often preferred to anti-climax because it is more readable: it avoids tailing off. The story-teller wants you to keep asking 'What happened next?' You can sometimes use the tricks of the story-teller in an essay. But if leaving the most important points (problems, solutions) till last produces suspense bordering on confusion, then you should sacrifice readability to clarity. In an essay you cannot afford to make the experiments that feature writers make in magazine articles, for example using a fictional technique like creating suspense to increase the drama of a situation.

Example
Such a topic as 'How does Celie's character change from an oppressed teenager to an independent woman through *The Colour Purple*?' demands an expository essay built on a narrative framework.

HOW TO DESCRIBE

As an essay topic instruction, **describe** means, as already noted, 'give a detailed account', discuss, as well as what it normally means. For example:

> Describe the administration of your school
> (or university, college, place of work).

or:

> Describe the functions and procedures of the
> Parliamentary Committees of Inquiry.

Pure description may be found in scientific essays (biology for example), although usually combined with exposition.

Being systematic

When describing, choose carefully the order of details. You need to give the reader a picture of the object or a clear pattern of the process. Chronological order may be involved. You may need to record the way something changes in the course of time (classrooms becoming more technological; a landscape seen from a moving train). A town may need space order ('to the north . . . to the south . . . in the middle . . . round this . . . in the outskirts . . .').

Making a word picture

To describe well in the more usual meaning of the term — to draw or paint an object, place, scene or person so that the reader sees it (smells it, and so on) — requires imagination and observational powers. These come through in vivid imagery and style with some originality. Such description is aimed at in creative essays and in incidental parts of others.

Nouns and **verbs** are as important as adjectives and adverbs. The latter must be chosen carefully so that your essay is not slowed down.

HOW TO ANALYSE AND EXPLAIN

Most essays are analytical in part, many are largely so. Get to know the different patterns expected by the various instructions you will meet. The following are quick, rough guides. Consider how they can be adapted to particular essay topics:

Analyse: Break up into its parts or aspects or periods. Examine the merits and defects, or successes and failures.

Define, and clarify: Say exactly what it is. Correct misconceptions. Say what it isn't.

Compare: Say in what ways things are similar. Explain an unfamiliar object or idea by saying how it compares with an object or idea that is familiar.

Do you want your reader to remember your abstract explanations or arguments? Then provide examples — illustrations, anecdotes and analogies, or extended comparisons. In other words, translate abstract into concrete so that the reader can picture it. For example, you illustrate a famine with figures of people starving set against the amount of food available. An anecdote about Napoleon can give an insight into his character or achievement. You may want to explain how the brain works by using the analogy of a sophisticated machine.

Contrast:	Explain how things actually differ that have similarities.
Assess:	Give the pluses and minuses; sum up on the value.
Explain:	Give causes of or reasons for.
	Show how it has become what it is.
	Show why it behaves as it does.

Be complete

Your exposition has to be knowledgeable so that the reader is prepared to believe what you say. It must also be complete, for if a gap is noticed, your credibility will suffer.

Using creative exposition

Instructions will sometimes demand some creativity in the way you approach the topic, but this is not always obvious. Consider, for example, how the essay on Cromwell was approached: the way the historical figures were recreated in the imagination (see page 53).

Example

Examples of creative exposition at GCSE level are such coursework 'empathy' assignments as the following (suggested as a guide by Southern Examining Group):

> From the late 18th century there were demands for the abolition of slavery in the British Empire. Describe and explain the differing reactions of people in Britain to these demands.

Empathy assignments have as their aim 'to show an understanding of the points of view held by people in the past and to explain why they held them'.

The kind of information you are specifically looking for here is opinions, rather than character traits. A literary topic sometimes wants you to imagine yourself inside the author's or fictional character's head to reproduce the author's kind of creativity. (This is especially so if the novel is psychological, and the reader is put into the protagonist's head from the word go, as happens with *Jane Eyre* and *The Colour Purple*.) The kind of imagination sometimes wanted by a history topic, in contrast, is your *historical* imagination. Can you relate those opinions, feelings, reactions . . . to historical facts? Of course the two kinds of imagination have much more in common, but it is important to get the emphasis right, to harness the imagination to the discipline.

HOW TO ARGUE

What arguing means
To argue means to maintain by reasoning, to prove, to persuade. Before you argue, you generally have to clear the ground by some analysis, especially by:

● defining terms
● clarifying issues
● removing misconceptions.

There were several examples of this process in Chapter 4. Note that it is usually reasonable to set a limit when defining what most people would mean by a 'term' – you might decide that 'adults' in your essay means anyone who has finished school education; 'tragedy' in a literature essay might require a classical or a modern definition.

Inducing and deducing
There are two main kinds of reasoning: **induction** and **deduction**.

Induction
Induction means arguing **from the particular to the general**. For example, you suggest that because Birmingham's citizens are increasingly worried about pollution of the atmosphere, and because Birmingham is an average city, then the citizens of Britain's other cities will feel the same. The argument will only be as valid as your evidence. If Birmingham, in fact, is likely to suffer much more from pollution than other cities, your argument tends to collapse.

Deduction
Deduction means arguing **from the general to the particular**. As long as the general rule that you are basing your deduction on is well proven,

the deduction is certain. For example: all cities contain a fair number of criminals. Birmingham is a city. Therefore Birmingham contains a fair number of criminals.

Beware of fallacies!
A deduction such as this, in three parts, is called a **syllogism**: major premise, minor premise and conclusion. A **fallacy** — a flawed or misleading argument — occurs when your major premise is false. For example: all Scotsmen are mean; John McGregor is a Scotsman; therefore John McGregor is mean. The reasoning process is valid, but the initial assumption is wrong.

A fallacy also occurs when the middle term doesn't follow the rules of logic, so that the conclusion doesn't necessarily follow. As in: Mentally ill people behave irrationally. John McGregor behaves irrationally. Therefore John McGregor is mentally ill. 'Behaving irrationally' in the minor premise does not have the same meaning as it does in the major premise. Call these false syllogisms.

Reasoning clearly
Practise thinking clearly when in discussions with friends:

● What exactly do you mean by that term?

● What is the evidence for that statement?

● Aren't you offering an opinion as if it were a fact?

● Is the argument valid but the assumption wrong?

● Is it a case of bias — 'you would say that, wouldn't you?'

But show your even-handedness by subjecting your own arguments to the same scrutiny. To maintain by reasoning means to produce convincing evidence, in the form of facts and informed (expert) opinions, to back up your beliefs.

The place for emotion in argument
To argue you need to be able to:

— reason well (think clearly)
— weigh evidence coolly

— come to well-considered conclusions.

But the aim is to persuade, and emotion has its place in making the reader receptive to your reasoning. An essay on the homeless or on drug addiction will benefit from some attempt to get the reader sympathetic to the plight of the sufferers, especially at the start, to grab attention. Talking about literature is unthinkable without feeling.

In essays in the '-ologies', on the other hand, emotion may be out of place — directly exploited emotion certainly is. When aiming to be as objective as possible, you should be aware of exactly how emotion is operating in anything you write.

Your head must rule your heart in any essay, otherwise there will be serious flaws in your argument. Since flaws in an argument tend to be unconscious, show your work to your sharpest critic. Give that critic room in your head when you write. Chapter 7 describes the various kinds of flaws in argument and explains how to detect them.

FITTING A PATTERN TO YOUR SUBJECT

Different patterns, we have seen, cut across each other. For example, 'What were the causes of the First World War?' would have its chronological patterns broken into separate aspects — political, economic, and so on.

Essays on literature often require careful consideration of patterns. 'Trace the changes in Bernard Shaw's dramatic art by comparing and contrasting early, middle and late periods' suggests chronological order.

But many variations would be possible. For example:

● You could keep to the **chronological** basis suggested by the title. You could divide the essay into three main sections: early, middle and late. You could take one or two representative texts in each period, analysing each under such aspects as theme, plot, characterisation, language. You would note the changes in the author's art as you went, and sum up with your conclusions at the end.

● You could build each section round an **aspect** rather than round the period: four main sections rather than three. Thus you would trace the changes in the way Shaw dealt with themes right through the representative texts of each period, then plot, then characterisation, then language.

● You would decide how to slot into these patterns your **viewpoint** (or thesis), the objections (or antithesis), and your considered conclusion (or synthesis). In other words, you might draw together the main arguments at the end of each section, or leave the synthesis largely to the end of the essay.

Building to a climax

The main patterns of argument have been covered under exposition. Note that climax order, with its variations, is generally more satisfying; it is more likely to hold the reader's interest than anti-climax. It has been pointed out that climax — with the sense of keeping the important till last — is not often suitable for down-to-earth, straightforward reports and investigations. But these will often use the variations of climax: for example, moving from the simple to the complex, or moving from the familiar to the unfamiliar.

SLOTTING IN YOUR EVIDENCE

In both exposition and argument, you need to produce your evidence for your statements. This evidence has to be smoothly written in, otherwise your line of development will be blurred. Slot the references (exact quotes or quotations, or particular statements/opinions) into your plan: author, title, page number will suffice.

Example

A section of a plan for an essay in psychology reads:

> *Variations between scientific and commonsense approaches*
> Some areas of study less scientific, *eg* Freud.
> Pure scientific method, *eg* Skinner.
> More flexible approach, *eg* Piaget.
> (The Bibliography is given at the end, with details of texts.)

There is sufficient linkage in the words, 'less', 'pure', and 'more' to suggest how to write it up. Let's see, in fact, how the linking sentences worked:

> Some psychologists, such as Freud, seem to have been less concerned with a rigorous scientific approach . . . At the other extreme, some behaviourist psychologists, such as Watson and Skinner, rejected all but strictly scientific methods of studying human behaviour . . .

(It was decided that Piaget needed a new paragraph:)
Perhaps a more typical approach for psychologists combines commonsense with science . . . Piaget seems to provide an example of this more flexible approach . . .

USING ANECDOTES, QUOTES AND QUOTATIONS

Used well, these elements can give an essay a lift.

Anecdotes

These are short, true stories, which are interesting or striking, and may be funny. They are a lively way of illustrating a point. They bring real life people into an otherwise abstract discussion. An anecdote about a parliamentary candidate being interviewed in his/her constituency, for example, may be a good way of revealing aspects of the interview procedure.

Quotes

Here we mean the exact words of someone interviewed — whether by yourself or an author; or extracts from published material. In a psychology essay, you quote Freud, *etc* and commentators.

Quotations

These are the well-known brief extracts from the statements of the famous, and for well-known extracts from literature. The first kind can be used to inject some humour, wit, or vivid image into an essay. For example, you might want to use the one enshrined in an anecdote about the American wit Dorothy Parker: when told that President Coolidge (a quiet man) was dead, she said, 'How can they tell?' But some quotations such as Winston Churchill saying during the Second World War, 'We will fight in the streets . . .' may be too well known.

Quotations from literature, as used for discussion points for some of the chapters of this book, can quickly add resonance or an extra dimension to your thoughts. But avoid, again, the too well known.

Both quotes and quotations must be used to support your points and must be directly relevant to the topic, not used for their own sake.

Using quotes as evidence

In literature essays your quotes (from published commentaries) and quotations (from studied texts) are key parts of the evidence for your interpretation or argument. Essays in psychology and sociology and others, which need to 'compare and contrast' the work of several authorities, may have to be content with brief statements of their positions rather than quotes. You may be expected to give title and page number for reference. Quotes from newspaper articles can be effective when dealing with current affairs.

Memory checks

(a) Define 'analogy' and give an example. Then compare with what is said on page 80–81.

(b) Define 'induction' and 'deduction', giving an example of each. Then compare with page 82.

TASK (Try to complete in 20 minutes)

The following sentences have come from essays. Rewrite them to make the meaning clearer.

1. She told the girl in Reception that the manageress was upset by the remarks that she had made to her.

2. One or two of the largest local authorities are employing on their staff as certifying officers and advisers to the Race Relations Act Committees officers having special qualifications or experience in race relations.

3. Flexibility is one of the lynch-pins of programme-budgeting.

4. The road from A to B has not yet got off the ground.

5. The New Scottish Nation Movement may be non-sectarian: it is playing straight into the hands of those who are.

6. In selection procedures the assumption was made that little weight would be attached to the matter of polished manners. Why on earth not? was the question raised in some quarters.

7. The goal aimed at by this particular company was undoubtedly optimum communication in terms of understanding and response rather than the stimulation of imaginative kinds of speculation about the future.

8. The achievement of an increase in the speed of the machine was effected by the operator applying pressure to the foot pedal.

9. They agreed to the recommendation of the local council department which was extremely short-sighted.

10. There is no reason whatsoever to doubt that what Henry VIII said was not true.

SUMMARY

Giving your essay conviction means that the reader is assured that your account is clear and accurate. Your point of view, even if disagreed with, will be sufficiently backed up by evidence.

Handling narration

Chronological order may be cut across by expository order. Climax order is usually more readable than anti-climax. Clarity is the criterion rather than readability. Verbs are used to carry forward an account concisely.

Handling description

A detailed account requires careful order of details to give a framework easily grasped by the reader. Creative description involves the five senses. Generally, use nouns and verbs rather than adjectives and adverbs. Use the second pair in creative essays but with as much originality as possible. Don't let them slow down the pace.

Handling exposition

First you need to analyse: divide the subject into its parts or aspects, so that it can be examined. To 'explain' means to give causes or reasons for. You may need to define, compare, contrast, and assess. **Creative exposition** using your historical imagination is required by some history topics. It is often required in essays on literature, to respond to the creativity of the authors studied. When some creativity of approach or expression is demanded by a topic, be careful to harness it to the discipline.

Handling argument

To 'argue' means to maintain by reason – prove – persuade. Clear the ground by analysis and explanation — for example, by defining terms. Use induction (arguing from the particular to the general) and deduction (arguing from the general to the particular). Back up your points by evidence of facts and expert opinions. Use persuasive power appealing to feelings when necessary as well as reasoning, but aim at objectivity in science subjects.

Checklist for a sound argument

● Is it clear what the proposition is – what exactly is being argued?

● Are sources given for facts that might be questioned?

● Are opinions based on facts?

● Are there factual errors?

● Is there a lack of facts and figures?

● Are the points made in logical order?

● Does the reasoning convince, or are there flaws in it?

Noting your evidence

Insert references into notes and show links, to help the writing up. Quotes and quotations, used as evidence, must be directly relevant to the topic.

7

How to Think Straight and Argue Well

'I am firm, you are obstinate, he is pig-headed.'
An often used illustration of how emotional words and phrases prevent us from
thinking objectively

There is, of course, a place for emotion in argument – it can play an
important part in persuasion. The case study on pages 102–104 illustrates this. But this chapter has to be mainly concerned with showing
how unsound reasoning (or 'crooked thinking') is sometimes difficult to
detect, and by giving you some effective techniques for detecting it.
Having read through the various flaws listed, go through them again,
testing yourself by covering up the comments to see if you can reproduce them. Wherever your comment on the example would differ, try to
work out why, and discuss it with colleague or tutor. Differing from the
comments given doesn't necessarily mean that you are wrong.

COMMON FLAWS IN ARGUMENT

The examples of flaws given below are expressed in their simplest
forms, so that the points made will be clear. To detect such flaws in
your thinking and writing, it's a good idea to test your reasoning in
discussion with others of different views.

False syllogisms and other fallacies

False syllogisms take many different forms. Here are two others to add
to those given on page 83.

The either-or fallacy or false dilemma
Example: 'Either she knew exactly what she was doing when she
murdered her husband or she is insane.'

Comment: In a court of law, the experts are wheeled in to assess whether
she should go to prison or a mental hospital, and it is often difficult to

make that assessment. Where do you draw the line between sanity and insanity? Such words, when used in an argument, need careful definition, so that your audience knows exactly where you stand.

Conclusion unjustified by the evidence:
Example: 'He said that if he was promoted to manager he would move to a new house. He did move to a new house. So he was promoted to manager.'
Comment: His aunt, of course, may have died and left him the house in her will.

Such conclusions are sometimes expressed as: 'So he *must have been* promoted to manager'. When you find yourself using such phrases as 'must have been' you know there's a doubt in your mind that you must try to remove. We have seen that a valid argument can lead to a false conclusion when the assumption was false. Now we find that a flawed argument, a faulty connection, can lead to a true conclusion. We are concerned with the flaw in the argument: it's not enough that what you're arguing is true. You must convince by sound reasoning.

Begging the question
Assuming to be true what you're supposed to be proving.

Example: 'Sending more criminals to prison will decrease crime.'

Comment: Perhaps in the short term it will, but prison is notoriously a good place to learn how to be a more effective criminal.

Bias, or sweeping generalisation
Ignoring the facts, especially those that support the opposing argument.

Example: 'Undoubtedly violence on TV is responsible for much of the violence in the streets.'

Comment: The use of persuader words such as 'undoubtedly' without finding evidence implies that there is no case to answer. Other persuaders used in this way are 'clearly', 'plainly', 'obviously', 'surely'. The arguer may be fully persuaded, or too lazy to think it out, or dishonestly trying to browbeat any opponent.

Example: 'The Labour Party are purely interested in getting elected and will make any kind of promises to secure that end' or 'The Conservative Party are only interested in ensuring that the rich stay rich and all the tax changes they make favour the top rather than the bottom rung of society.'

Comment: Such statements, particularly common in politics, suffer from what may be called the 'all for some' fallacy. There is *some* truth in them, but what is badly needed is an indication of *how much*. What is needed is evidence in the shape of facts and figures (expertly gathered statistics if the issue is complex). By using the abstractions 'Labour Party' or 'Conservative Party' you can make your arguments usefully vague, less easy to pin down. Note the extremism of 'purely' and 'any kind' in the first statement, and of 'only' and 'all' in the second. Other words to watch are superlatives ('the best solution'), and other adverbs that do the work of 'purely' here are 'always', 'never', 'everywhere', 'nowhere'.

Emotionally weighted and prejudiced language

When the facts are not sufficient evidence for a strongly held belief, there is a tendency to fill the gap with rousing words, or to rationalise, which means to support a belief on irrational grounds. Allow others, in discussion, to help you to detect such tendencies.

Example (from a student's essay):

Some people merely call them unemployed; I call them work-shy. I believe my grandfather is right. He says that his generation was brought up to believe that you had to make your own way in the world, that the world didn't owe you a living. The young school leavers today are mostly layabouts, not interested in work. They are not willing to take on any responsibilities. They are lazy, bad mannered, and indifferent to anything outside their own contentment.

Comment: If you find yourself arguing angrily or with emotion like this, test your argument by replacing highly charged language with neutral words. Here you would replace 'work-shy' (unmotivated), 'layabouts' (idle?), 'lazy', 'bad-mannered'. If your rewritten piece does not contain good evidence, it was depending on emotion instead of fact. You will have to think again, and straight this time, before rewriting.

Special pleading

Example: You argue that tax benefits should be increased for private schools. You may or may not recognise that your argument is motivated by your own advantage. Your father is proprietor and headmaster of a private school, and you expect to follow in the same career.

Comment: We are all likely to get involved in a discussion or an essay where special pleading is a danger for us. An extra effort is then required to see the opposing point of view.

Unexamined analogies

On page 81 it was suggested that if you need to explain something fairly complex, an analogy, or extended comparison, may be useful. But don't push an analogy too far.

Make sure you know all you need to know about the two things you are comparing (especially if you refer to computers, which are becoming more sophisticated by the minute). The things being compared may have four qualities in common but that doesn't guarantee that a fifth quality in one will be matched by the other.

Non-sequiturs and red herrings

'Non-sequitur' is Latin for 'it doesn't follow'.

Example: 'When he was President, the country suffered its worst slump. Clearly he was an ineffective President.'

A 'red herring' is a similar confusion, perhaps more deliberate.
Example: 'She could not have murdered her husband. To realise that, you only have to see how kind she is to animals.'

Appeals to authority or tradition

Authority

You may quote a scientist — preferably two — on a scientific matter as part of your evidence. Don't quote a scientist, however famous, to back up a point about literature.

Example: 'I'm not alone in believing that Shakespeare is over-rated. Professor Harrington, Professor of Physics at Longwayout University, said exactly the same thing in a television interview.'

Comment: Remember that even two Professors of English Literature can have quite different views on a particular author's merits.

Tradition

Authority and tradition are combined in the example for emotionally weighted language. Grandfather may well be worth listening to on the subject of morality and good character, but he may not be an authority on the employment prospects for school leavers today, and his view should be compared with other evidence. 'It has always been done this way' doesn't mean that a better way has not been found.

Language lacking precision

Imprecise language weakens an argument. If you are clear in what you want to say, the clear words should come. (See Chapter 9.)

CASE STUDIES

The case studies that follow are designed to illustrate how valuable discussion (for the tutor as much as for the student) can be when flaws that are difficult for the arguer to detect creep into arguments.

Neil's thought habits are examined

Neil
You must admit, sir, that there are some very weird customs in some countries. I was only saying that the British Empire brought civilisation to savage peoples.

Tutor
You will have to define 'civilisation'. The question says, **'Was the British Empire good for Africa?'** — so you've introduced the term. It's a word that's been much abused, don't you agree? Don't forget to look at those 'weird customs', as you call them, from the Africans' point of view. You'll find that there is often a civilised system as the framework for them.

Neil
I don't see anything civilised about female circumcision.

Tutor
No. I'll leave that question for a moment. But don't have too narrow an idea of what civilisation means. All nations have customs unique to themselves which seem strange or absurd to other nations. It's what makes the world an interesting place, isn't it?

Neil
Like teachers saying all these students want is entertainment.

Tutor
Yes. [*Laughs.*] Or students saying all teachers are interested in is league tables. If we're feeling mentally tired or lazy, it's hard to put a lot of thought into a discussion, whether orally or in an essay. The danger is that we just reach into our minds and take what's already there on the shelves, so to speak. What do we find there?

Neil
Tins of beans? [*Laughs*]. Sorry. You were talking the other day about predigested thinking. Is that what you mean?

Tutor
Exactly. Or thought habits. Reaching for ready-made or predigested

thoughts that save us the trouble of thinking for ourselves. All right. Tins of beans if you like. Instead of planning a meal with a cook book, shopping for the right ingredients, spending time on preparing and cooking.

Neil
It's quite a good analogy, sir, for writing an essay.

Tutor
I was hoping you'd say that . . . Not perfect, but it'll do. Then of course there are slogans . . .

Neil
Life is better under the Conservatives. Or Labour isn't working.

Tutor
What they hope is that the repetition all over the place in posters or in TV adverts will make the words repeat themselves in our minds, so that we can't hear the opposite view.

Neil
Brainwashing, innit? Isn't it?

Tutor
To get back to your essay. Visitors from abroad, probably bringing their 'weird customs' with them, are delighted by many things in this 'civilised' country. The British Museum, the Houses of Parliament, the charming, good-mannered way we queue up for buses. But they are shocked to see young people begging in the shop doorway opposite the bus-stop. Try to look at your own country like a visitor and another country like a native. There's the clue to getting out of bad thought habits.

Neil
And don't eat too many beans.

Marjorie has her assumptions questioned

The Sociology teacher has found time to discuss with her class, one by one, their plans and rough drafts for an essay on **'On balance, do you think the mentally ill should be cared for in the community? What problems is this policy confronting?'**

Tutor
What you've written is very interesting, Marjorie. It needs to focus more on the question. I like the examples you find to illustrate your points. The story of the woman in the film for instance. *An Angel at my Table*: it sounds like a good film. She was in a mental hospital for

years and finally got out by proving everybody wrong by publishing books. But your essay is becoming 'Is there such a thing as mental illness?'

Marjorie

What I meant was that there's no exact line that can be drawn between a person who is mentally ill and someone who is not. She was misdiagnosed as schizophrenic. And you realise that if the experts can get it wrong . . .

Tutor

If the experts can get it wrong we have to know how to balance one expert against another. We must question the assumptions of experts as well as each other's. That's a theme we must return to. Now you make a good case for treating the large majority of the mentally ill in the community. But you've taken it a bit too far, haven't you? I think you extend it to fit that other title I mentioned. You treat the problems at the end, the lack of coordination between the different authorities, and so on, but very sketchily.

Marjorie

I did mention the man who warned he was going to murder somebody if they let him out. And they did let him out. And he did murder someone. But there are ten times more people murdered by so-called sane people than by so-called mentally ill people aren't there?

Tutor

For the purposes of argument in an essay you've got to provide a serviceable definition of such key terms as 'mentally ill' that fits the context. Especially here where you're asked to consider practical problems. Suppose it's *your* decision to say yes or no: do I let this person out of my mental hospital or not? Will he be a danger to himself, or to others? Then you might be inclined to say: no, he won't be a danger. But perhaps there won't be sufficient support out there for this person's type of illness? Apart from this business of the various authorities, the local councils, the day centres, the GPs *etc* . . .

Marjorie

He might not have a family ready to help him or friends, or people prepared to give him a job.

Tutor

That's it. To get back to those murders. Of course there are many more murders committed by sane people than there are by insane people. But could you have another think about that? What exactly does it prove?

Marjorie
Well, I suppose there are more murders by sane people because there are ten times as many sane people as people who are mentally ill. Or there may be 20 times as many. That was stupid, wasn't it? I was trying to say there's a lot prejudice against mentally ill people by people who don't understand it, and they imagine they're all dangerously violent. In fact you'd have to compare the proportion who are dangerously violent against the proportion of sane people who are.

Tutor
That's a very good point. I'm going to provide the class with some statistics to draw on, which might help there. And we're going to work out together one or two definitions of 'mentally ill' that we can all agree with. If a man decides to grow a beard, is there a precise day on which he can be described as 'bearded'?

Marjorie
What? [*Smiles.*] Oh, you're talking about George. He gave up, sir, he shaved it off.

Tutor
Not George. Anybody. This is important. He allows to grow, let's say, one hair each day. Where do you draw the line between him being not bearded and being bearded. If the 27th day, why not the 25th day, or the 29th day?

Marjorie
Oh, I get it. Do you know what we called George? Follically challenged.

Walter is warned about 'scoring points'

Walter was not pleased with Dr June Inge's comments on his Political Theory essay: **'Identify some ambiguities in politicians' use of words and indicate where you think they may be excusable. Illustrate your points by examples from both past and present.'**

The comment has been festering in his mind at work, and a colleague had asked him, 'Who are you thinking of murdering today?' Now, after a good dinner and half a bottle of wine he didn't feel any friendlier towards the world.

His wife said, 'You'd better read it out. It will get it off your chest.'

He took the essay and the tutor's typed report out of the envelope and read:

Dear Walter
I've given you C+ for this essay and I do realise you will be disappointed with the grade. You have obviously worked very hard on this

essay and in many ways it shows promise. You have provided many revealing examples of the ambiguous language of politicians past and present. You found some interesting examples of blatantly dishonest arguing by politicians, notably that quoted by Susan Stebbing in that old classic, *Thinking To Some Purpose* . . . Etcetera.

'What was that case quoted?' Mrs Jeffrey asked.

'He was director of an armaments company and there was an inquiry into the trade. This was way back in 1934 before the Second World War. Things don't change much, do they? The company director was asked: did he really think his products were no more dangerous or obnoxious than boxes of chocolates or sugar candy — or children's crackers? So he said, "Well, I nearly lost an eye with a Christmas cracker, but never with a gun."

'Anyway, she's apparently so pleased with me. She goes on: You pick up these two examples of crooked argument here — the getting away from the point with the feeble joke, and the fact that the comparison is not valid — armaments are made to kill and injure, and crackers are not. And you find other crooked arguments equally illuminating . . .

'She praises one or two others . . . Then . . . here we go . . .

Unfortunately, you spend too long on the more obvious dishonesties. When you come to the more subtle ambiguities you make too many allowances. You take at their face value and defend, for example, government ministers' statements that too much time for leisure and educational activities in prisons is not desirable . . .

Mrs Jeffrey said, 'Who said it *was* desirable? Too much leisure?'

'Nobody. But quite a number of lefties have been saying there should be more time devoted to education and leisure. The idea of punishment in prisons is disappearing altogether, for Godsake.'

'Wait a minute.' Mrs Jeffrey slowly and carefully replaced her coffee cup in the saucer. 'Leave aside the question of punishment for the moment. What those lefties, as you call 'em, are saying is that there's a right amount, an appropriate amount, of time for these things. And that in their view it is not, on the whole, enough. "Too much" of anything means bad. But no one is arguing "too much" of anything is good. So you are extending the opposite argument. That's trickery on your part. A form of begging the question which is deliberate rather than accidental. I call it blatant dishonesty on your part, darling. Now about this matter of punishment.'

'Punishment?' Walter cried. 'Haven't I been punished enough? And I came to you for sympathy.'

Christine has to separate words from facts

Christine
Sir, you've written here, 'What do you mean by "non-intervention"?' You know, not intervening, not taking any side in the war.

Tutor
The trouble with that particular war, though, was that it went on for several years, and the British Government's policy shifted as first one side, then the other, seemed to be winning.

Christine
We still kept out of it though, didn't we?

Tutor
Yes, but those shifts in policy were important to the question. And in any case, there was a difference in the attitudes of the two main parties. If I oversimplify it, I think you'll see what I mean. Let's call it Left fighting Right in the civil war in Politavia. At first the Left were winning. In Britain the Left party argued that we should have a policy of non-intervention. Why, do you think?

Christine
Because they wanted the Left in Politavia to win.

Tutor
Exactly. What this meant, in effect, was intervention on the side it wanted to win. It's just that they don't say 'non-intervention on the side of . . .' Not doing anything can be just as influential as doing something. Remember what we said about voting in an election.

Christine
Oh yeah, if too many of a party's supporters don't bother to vote because it's raining or something, they may be letting the other party win.

Tutor
Meanwhile, back in Politavia — the Right in Britain, which is the Government, are preparing a policy of intervention — on which side?

Christine
On the side of the Right in Politavia.

Tutor
While the parties in this country are still arguing about it, the Right in Politavia suddenly take the upper hand. Now what is the Government in Britain saying?

Christine
Non-intervention.

Tutor
And the Left party in Britain?

Christine
They'd like to intervene against the Right.

Tutor
That's all grossly oversimplified, of course. But it makes the point that 'non-intervention' is one of those words used by politicians especially that need careful scrutiny. And careful handling in essays. A powerful government will say they can't intervene in a country where there's an oppressive regime on the grounds that they can't disturb national sovereignty. On the other hand, you may find the same powerful government *will* intervene in another country having a similar regime. Why? It could be that they won't intervene where there's an alliance or an association of some kind. They've been friendly for a long time.

Christine
There could be a lot of trade between them. And very little trade with the other country.

Tutor
So you've got to notice not only the words that governments use but also the facts they're supposed to be describing. You've got to look at the words and facts separately and see if they match up.

Christine
On the other hand, you can't sit on the fence arguing about the meanings of words if you're being bombed to smithereens.

Tutor
That's a good point, Christine. It there weren't some slogan-making at times of war or at election time, people might be paralysed by indecision.

Christine
But in essays you've got to look at everything critically. Without a gun to your head.

Tutor
We're getting on to the same wave-length, aren't we?

David wants to be judge and jury

David has decided to go on to university and study law. He is finding that both in his Law and Government course and in his Political Studies course he is becoming impatient with anything he finds in the media that is not the truth, the whole truth and nothing but the truth. This impatience, his tutor points out, is the cause of some unhelpful digression in an essay on Law and Government.

David
It's the lies in the papers that bug me. And the lack of proportion, which sometimes is the same as lying. I mean, I do check papers with different politics against each other, when I have time.

Tutor
Try *The Week* and other weekly reviews. Skim through them and photo-copy the odd article.

David
Even in those weeklies, it's circumstantial evidence, isn't it?

Tutor
Can you define 'circumstantial evidence' for me?

David
It's a number of facts which, when you add them up, appear to prove a certain conclusion. But any one fact wouldn't prove that conclusion.

Tutor
That's fair enough. Now the media no doubt is purveying much circum-stantial evidence. News stories can run and run. New evidence for a run-ning story arrives for every issue or every broadcast. Journalists have to be thinking on the hoof They can't be saying 'as far as we know' at the start of every sentence. How do we get a balanced view?

David
[*Rifles through his course notes.*] It says here in my class notes: Readers must do three things. One, avoid own mistakes of observation and interpre-tation. Two, see where reports contain such mistakes and identify preju-dices, bias, *etc*. Three, identify dishonesties, *eg* of extremists, Right or Left.

Tutor
Good. And you could have done it without looking at your notes.

David
Of course. But when you're quoting the experts . . .

Tutor
OK. Now without looking at your notes, David. In a court of law there are

various bodies and procedures that help to ascertain the truth that readers of books or newspaper articles don't have at their disposal. You're sitting in the gallery for a serious criminal case. What is it that helps you?

David
Right, well yes. You've got a judge for a start. You've got a jury. You've got counsel for the prosecution. You've got counsel for the defence. Statements — that is, evidence from the accused and witnesses for and against.

Tutor
Of course, things can still go wrong. People may lie and be believed. But with all these checks and balances . . . The point is, when we write anything, and when we read anything, we don't get all that help. We're not in a court of law.

David
Never again will I mention circumstantial evidence, outside of a court of law.

Tutor
So we have to be content that writers get as near the truth they can in the time they have available. And when the Chancellor of the Exchequer says the economy is healthy . . .

David
I suppose he thinks, if I tell the whole truth, people will get scared and that will have a bad effect on the economy.

Tutor
He's defending a policy, understandable isn't it? The opposition's job is to monitor the Government's administration, criticise the policy when necessary. I suppose we'd better say, as often as they can. That's politics.

David
[*Laughs.*] It ain't the truth, but it's politics.

Ann is told to start shocking people

Ann was astonished. Was her Psychology tutor heading for a breakdown? Too much study of Psychology, perhaps, is dangerous. Yet she looked just the same, with her calm, modulated voice and reassuring granny glasses. Did she really say, 'You've got to start shocking people'?

Ann
But you're always saying: reason carefully, make sure you're taking

your readers with you. Your essays are too emotional and sound too much like speeches, you used to say.

Tutor

Perhaps I've overstressed the cool reasoning side of things. When you're asked to compare quotations from Piaget with one or two other educational theorists you have to keep close to the texts. But for '**Is our educational system out of date?**' you can be more forthright. Which points do you feel most strongly about?

Ann

I suppose . . . ideas about how young people can learn to live in a multicultural society, the way the likely work patterns of the future are not being anticipated . . .

Tutor

You could say more about these areas. And strongly. Why aren't these ideas given more emphasis by educators?

Ann

Ingrained habits of thought. Unconscious habits — that come from their class, and upbringing, their nationality, and so on.

Tutor

Yes. Attack them. You've rather too much of the 'perhaps one should be rather less narrow . . .' Then I'd like to see you move quicker from the need for people to open up their minds to face the future, to how the educational system should encourage it. You say creativity is often discouraged at an early age — because of exams and league tables, and so on. We want more there on how to deal with this. Abolish league tables altogether?

Ann

Have exams that test originality as well as what you've swotted up. I want to put more about visual education and computers — how we should be more prepared for what computers will be ready to do.

Tutor

Even sometimes making outrageous speculations and seeing where they lead you. You can explain in your essay what you're doing, so that it doesn't sound crazy. Think of Darwin.

Ann

And Einstein. Didn't he say that although the angles of all the triangles ever met added up to two right angles, what if they didn't? And just asking that led him on to the theory of relativity.

Tutor

Quite. Yes, that's good. Check such statements in an encyclopedia or something, or say: 'I believe Einstein . . . etcetera, etcetera . . .' Of course, you can't set out to build a new educational system that will produce more Darwins and Shakespeares.

Ann

Why not?

[*Pause*]

Tutor

That's a point. Why not? Good. Just you keep asking why not.

TASK

Point out any exaggerations or faulty reasoning in the following extracts from essays. If you think any of the exaggerations may have been justified by what followed, explain that point of view.

1. In the United States there is the Pulitzer Prize, in Norway the Nobel Prize, in the UK there is Who wants to be a Millionaire?

2. The trouble with television is that it cannot deal with intellectuals. You don't get a serious scientist explaining something in any depth. You get an eccentric making funny expressions and contortions.

3. The long-term unemployed inevitably turn to drug abuse or crime.

4. An increasing number of young people today are rejecting the rules and values of civilised society.

5. The comprehensive system thought up by Left-wing theorists has been proved a failure. It is time to restore the educational standards in the UK that made Britain great.

6. Most single mothers are teenagers who have become pregnant in order to stand a better chance of obtaining a council flat and housing benefit.

7. The EU and all its works are supported by people who lack strong feelings for their own nation, who lack personality and like to be told what to do. Obviously all the EU rules are eroding our freedom.

8. The Turks are aggressive. Aggressiveness can lead to cruelty. Therefore the Turks tend to be cruel.

9. There is little value in the popular press. It is entertainment rather

than news, and anyone who doesn't watch a great deal of television would find the constant references to the lifestyles of TV celebrities of minimal interest, if not meaningless.

10. The popular press in the UK is a unique contribution to the world's journalism. It communicates what it is essential to know of the political and cultural happenings of the nation simply, directly and readably to the vast majority of the newspaper-reading population.

11. All dogs are four-footed animals.
    Rover is a four-footed animal.
    Therefore Rover is a dog.

12. Tick the correct answer — (a) or (b):
    'Only those who were unprejudiced were convinced' means
    (a) everyone who was unprejudiced was convinced
    (b) all who were convinced were unprejudiced.

13. Suppose you read the following report in a newspaper:
    'Vaccination does not prevent small pox or make it milder if contracted. More young people die from vaccination than from smallpox, according to the latest figures from the . . . .'

    Assuming the second statement to be true, does that make the first statement true? If not, why not?

SUMMARY

- **Crooked thinking**, unsound reasoning and flaws in argument are three phrases that mean the same thing. The common flaws in argument should be detected in others' arguments and avoided in your own.

- **Tricks in arguing** may be conscious (dishonest) or unconscious. Tricks that have developed out of prejudice or at least strong views may be conscious at first, but may in time become unconscious: the arguer will find them difficult to detect and avoid.

- **Taking account of opposing views**, which requires imaginative sympathy, is necessary for arguing well.

- **Testing your arguments** in discussion before and after writing an essay will help you to avoid flaws and to argue with conviction.

8

Writing Introductions and Conclusions

'Begin at the beginning,' the King gravely, 'and go on till you come to the end, then stop,' Lewis Carroll, *Alice's Adventures in Wonderland.*

YOUR THREE-PART PLAN

For the purpose of this chapter we are setting aside the body of the essay in order to concentrate on the head and the feet. However, let's remind ourselves how they all fit together, so that we can put the body back in due course.

To summarise the connections made at the start of Chapter 5:

1. **Introduction:** explain the title and what you intend to show.

2. **Body:** develop explanation/argument demanded by the topic with ideas, opinions and facts.

3. **Conclusion:** show that you have dealt with the topic/answered the question.

What this chapter will show you

Introductions
This chapter will help you to write introductions that:

- go straight to the topic, defining key terms and clarifying issues
- show the way ahead, indicating themes, viewpoint, and structure
- provide any necessary background
- arouse interest.

Conclusions
This chapter will help you to write conclusions that:

● sum up well
● finish firmly.

Vetting your work
It will also suggest a vetting strategy to:

● check that the title's demands are met
● check that the essay's promises are fulfilled.

Introductions and conclusions vary greatly. They need special attention, for your personal contribution to the essay topic tends to be specially required in these places.

WRITING GOOD INTRODUCTIONS

Going straight to your topic
An essay topic is like an order from a customer for a product that you will create specially, like a suit made to measure or a custom-built car – not what *you* would like to *produce*, but what *the customer* would like to *get*. There are two sets of requirements: the specific ones of the title, shown by the key terms and instructions (Chapter 2), and the general requirements of the tutor.

Memory check
Write down what the tutor requires you to show in your essay. Check your points with the list on page 21.
   This chapter assumes that you have done all the thinking, planning (and possibly drafting). You know what the body says, or is to say, and therefore in what ways it meets those requirements.

Two introductions compared
Compare these two openings, for an essay entitled:

Are the national newspapers too biased in their reporting?

Judge them, making notes if you like, as you read, before comparing your assessment with the comments that follow.

Introduction A
   To be biased means that you are putting forward a distorted view of

a situation rather than a fair representation of the facts. Unless specifically stated to be a biased view the aim of the national newspaper is to report events as fairly as is reasonably possible and to support this with reasoned editorials where appropriate.

Unfortunately this is not always the case. Bias can creep into a news report at the reporting stage. The reporter is in a position to stress one side of the case far harder than the other. This may happen because the reporter has views on the subject himself or for reasons beyond his control, such as not being able to get all the facts he/she needs to be able to make a fair report.

Introduction B

Bias comes in two main forms. First, it is an influence on what is printed that is usually unfair but may be unconscious, for example when reporters do their best to give a fair account but (as is often the case) have not had time to collect all the facts. Secondly, the bias may come from prejudice, leading to conscious and blatant distortion, as when a racist publication withholds facts deliberately. I shall call these two forms weak and strong bias: they will be benchmarks in this attempt to answer the question.

Since complete objectivity is rare, I take the question to mean: Are national newspapers as fair and accurate as they should be — in other words, do they try hard enough? My view is that on the whole they do steer clear of strong bias, and I shall show how they resist the pressures. My main complaint is the way in which political views are often presented as facts.

Tutor's comment

Introduction A makes a fair attempt at defining bias and begins to explain the forces that make for bias in reporting. To that extent it goes straight to the topic in a businesslike way.

Its main fault is that it is not at all clear how the writer intends to answer the question. What kinds of bias will be discussed? What is the writer's own viewpoint?

It is also repetitive. The second sentence doesn't work because 'stated' is a disconnected particle: it is not the *aim* that is stated to be a biased view; and it is facts that support opinions, not the other way round. This makes for confusion. Read: 'Newspaper reporting should always aim at objectivity, and the facts should be used to support any opinion elsewhere — in leaders for example'.

Introduction B is a big improvement. It not only gives a clear and full definition of bias but shows how that will inform the essay as a whole. It shows what the writer understands by the title, the viewpoint and the approach to be followed — in other words, the way ahead. The tone is appropriately cool, as an argument essay's tone should be. To arouse more interest, a typical example of newspaper reporting bias, or a thought-provoking quote, might have helped both introductions.

Go for control, not display

To go *straight* forward shows that you are in confident control. Keep those doubts and uncertainties that lie at the heart of things until later, until your point of view is established.

Be confident, but not self-satisfied. Avoid a preamble that lines up concepts in a big-sounding way, but adds up to very little:

> A superficial reading of the text might deduce that the author is saying that political theories at this period were closer to the actual policies than at any other time perhaps in the history of the country. When one subjects the relevant passages to the more rigorous, in-depth analysis that they undoubtedly deserve. . .

Avoid also the pretentiousness of: 'Many critics have failed to understand that Shakespeare. . .' If you need to warm up in these ways, make sure you cut down when vetting your work.

Show your reader the way ahead

Indicate:

- the themes
- the viewpoint
- the structure.

to come. In its most explicit form, an introduction may be like a map of the area to be explored. It gives the main landmarks — the themes and ideas — in the order in which they will be reached. We have already had an example in Chapter 5 ('Extend paragraph to essay', page 68). A **summary paragraph** contained the points, or questions, that one by one the following paragraphs discussed.

The more formal essay in the social sciences might indicate detailed structure and verdict, as well as order of ideas. Its introduction might be more like a framework for a building than a map. Something like:

Four theories — A, B, C and D — will first be summarised, after which a comparative analysis will be made of them. I shall then be able to show why, in my view, the first theory works best as an explanation for the way the organisation functions as it does.

Explain your approach to the reader

This often means:

- interpreting the title's demands by defining terms
- showing how you intend to fulfil those demands.

Notice how Introduction B on page 108 does this; see how it goes on to clarify the issues further by explaining that two ends of the spectrum of bias would be benchmarks.

Defining your terms

We have seen several other examples of titles containing words that you need to define early on in your essay: 'children', 'corporal punishment', 'wisdom', 'wasted', 'old', and so on.

Defining the issues

You may have to identify right away the difficulties of carrying out what you have been asked to do, so that the reader is prepared for the battle ahead, as when terms in the topic have several possible definitions. You may be tempted to retort, as a famous professor did to most questions he was asked, 'It depends what you mean by — '.

People were reluctant to ask him 'How are you today?' fearing the reply, 'It depends what you mean by "how". And for that matter "are", "you", and "today". Could you please rephrase the question?'

You should resist the temptation to philosophise in this way. The first piece of advice, after all, was: go straight to the point.

Provide any necessary background

Example: history topic

Consider an A-Level History topic such as, 'How important were the policies of the Crown in causing rebellions from 1536 to 1554?' You would need to start by sketching in the situation in 1536. For example, explain how Henry VIII's disagreement with the Pope since his accession in 1509 had been alienating Roman Catholics. This would provide a suitable background against which you could go on to deal with the dissolution of the monasteries in 1536 and the start of the rebellions of Roman Catholics. Even so, your introduction would focus firmly on the connection between the early policies and the rebellions.

Example: literature topic
English Literature essays sometimes need historical background to put the topic in context. The changes in British attitudes to the French Revolution may need to be charted as context for some of the poetry of the time. Some biographical details might be needed as background to your discussion of a writer's work. You will judge how much background is needed and avoid digressing from your main purpose.

Arouse your reader's interest
The techniques of indicating precisely the order of the ideas to come illustrated above, with the four theories, carries the danger of dullness. So can devoting the introduction to explaining your approach. As in:

> The best approach to effective planning in industry is probably to make a careful study of typical examples of different phases of the planning problem.

That 'probably' may be wise academic caution, but did you feel a yawn coming on at that point in the sentence?
The dullness here is compounded by the plod of noun-plus-adjective clichés that dropped out of a mind on auto pilot.
Remember, tutors have many essays to read. They will feel well disposed towards the more readable essays, especially towards those whose introductions and conclusions stick in the mind. The more creative essays can borrow techniques for beginning and ending feature articles memorably.
Avoid, however, starting vividly and dramatically and then tailing off. Better a whimper and a bang than a bang and a whimper.
Techniques for arousing interest are:

Move from familiar to unfamiliar
Your introduction to a complicated subject (say, press freedom) will be clearer and more interesting if it leads the reader from the familiar to the less familiar – for example, from the right to criticise government policy to the intricacies of the law of libel.
An analogy often makes a useful introduction:

> Ironically, the animal whose name is a synonym for everything contemptible in the human vocabulary is in many essential respects the

most similar of all animals to man. The basis of this similarity is the fact that men and rats are the only omnivorous animals.

In this essay the analogy quickly builds a bridge from the familiar fact to the unfamiliar fact on which the theme is developed.

Move between concrete and abstract

You could begin an essay by saying that during the Second World War airmen came into a hospital badly injured. Or you could immediately make it concrete, to let the reader see it. You could, for example, tell an anecdote or relate a startling fact or statistic. An article in *The Mail on Sunday* begins:

> There were four ways in which airmen used to come into Ward 3 of the Queen Victoria Hospital in East Grinstead during the war: boiled, mashed, fried and roast. `Just like potatoes,' said one of them.

Use a quotation or a quote

Choose from books of quotations but make sure your choice is relevant to your subject. A student's essay on `What is education for?' begins:

> The 19th century philosopher Herbert Spencer gave a concise answer to this question, and it is an answer that appeals strongly to me. He said, 'Education has for its object the formation of character.' I believe its purpose is, or should be, to help us to develop the character and skills to live at peace and earn our living in the society we find ourselves in.

Note that this introduction both defines the key term 'character' and updates the associations. In other words it puts the quotation to work. Simply lacing your essay with quotations betrays a lack of confidence in what you have to say for yourself.

If sentimentality is one of the themes of your essay, you might dig out one or two pregnant quotations from your head or from a book. You might find 'A sentimentalist is one who desires the luxury of an emotion without paying for it' (Oscar Wilde) and:

> The rhetorician would deceive his neighbours,
> The sentimentalist himself . . . (W. B. Yeats)

Then you would ask yourself: which would best fit what I'm trying to say?, which most usefully develops a train of thought?, and: could I say it better myself? You might decide to use both quotations, probably in different places, but unless it's a long essay two quotations is probably your limit.

You can be more liberal with quotes. Discussing a politician of the past may need several quotes from his speeches.

Make the reader laugh or cry.
The above quote about the airman is enough to make you cry. Humour or wit can also make a point memorable. Avoid telling a joke for its own sake: it must be relevant and telling. A book of humorous quotations may produce something appropriate. Study humorous columnists.

WRITING GOOD CONCLUSIONS

Being firm
Be as firm as you can when you feel you have the evidence to back up your verdict or viewpoint. You will then be entitled to your opinion. Reasonableness doesn't mean bloodless. Provide a satisfying rounding-off, whether by a definite answer or by offering further food for thought.

Fake conclusions to avoid
Essay writers are sometimes tempted to fake a conclusion by:

● Suggesting that readers have been given a point of view to think about — *when they haven't.*

● Preaching in vague terms as if they had earned the right by producing evidence for their preaching — *when they haven't.*

● Following a line of reasoning not relevant to the topic — *and pretending that it is.* Sometimes they are deluding themselves; sometimes they hope that their writing skill will obscure the faking.

Coming to your final view
Summing up means pulling together the threads by connecting up the key points of the essay. Show that they finally add up to an explanation, opinion, judgement or proof — *more* than the sum of the parts.

Finishing strongly
Clinchingly
Finishing strongly means clinchingly — even dramatically and memo-

rably when that is appropriate — but without straining for effect. A good start or finish can be elusive when you are trying hard to find one.

Especially in creative essays, if you have a weak start and a strong finish, it can work well to transfer the finish to the start and rewrite the finish as an echo to the new start. Alternatively, a good start or finish may be lurking somewhere in your draft. It may need some tinkering with to get it right, of course. When you've moved it, make sure you fill the gap. End with a major point, not a minor one.

Speculatively
A firm finish can be achieved by adding something new, by looking into the future. Set the reader a new and important question or problem to think about, that will need to draw on the evidence or argument you have provided. You may be able to end with a new perspective on the topic, or speculate on future possibilities.

Anecdotally
Whether or not enshrined in a quote or quotation, an anecdote may make your ending vivid and memorable. Don't use one for both start and finish though. Overall, use such devices much more sparingly than journalists do. They must never be used for their own sake: always strictly relevant. An essay on:

Why do governments become bureaucratic?

begins: 'More and more people demand more and more from government', and ends: 'Bureaucracy tends to become in itself a government of too many people, by too many people, for too many people'. The witty adaption of a famous American quotation echoes the introduction and advances on it at the same time, well justified by what went between.

Vetting your draft conclusion
Seeing your essay as a whole, check your conclusion for the following:

1. It should normally be about the same **length**, or less than, the introduction. Together they should make up about a quarter of the whole essay.
2. Your conclusion should **move on** from the introduction, not merely repeat it.
3. Other people should have a **fair idea of the title** from your conclusion.

4. The conclusion should follow **inevitably** from title, introduction and body.

There should be a finality about it: a definite viewpoint if not an answer to a question or some kind of solution. At the least the conclusion should give your reader something definite to think about, and not merely tail off or stay in the air.

Vet your conclusion by reading it immediately after reading the introduction. Does it meet requirements 1 and 2 above? Vet the third requirement by asking a fellow-student to guess the title after you have read out the conclusion by itself.

Cover the conclusion, and read quickly through the introduction and body. Does something inevitably follow? Write it down. Then uncover what you wrote as a conclusion and compare.

Finally, could your conclusion be stronger than it is? Worse: have you produced a fake conclusion, in the hope that it will *appear* to meet the demand? Alternatively, the conclusion may be fair, but what goes before may be less satisfactory. In this case, rewrite the conclusion first, and keep it in front of you as a goal while you rewrite — a variation of the technique of conclusion first, the rest later, already discussed in Chapter 5.

TASK (30 minutes)

(A) *Rewrite this introduction to an essay on 'How equal are the women in the Armed Forces of the UK?' Reduce to about 160 words, to sharpen the focus. Avoid changing the subject so frequently.*

When you consider the Armed Forces today you might think about women but it's unlikely. You'll probably think about piles of rubble among huge fires or of grey deserts left by a nuclear holocaust. The British ships were full of men that beat back the Falkland invasion and there were pictures daily on television of the brave British soldiers and airmen who waged the war on Iraq. Going back into the past the impression is that women did in the Armed Forces the things they are traditionally expected to do. The nursing and the secretarial work and all that. Some people like to think of that support being there but other people say that war is a man's job and women shouldn't be there, except in peace time, because they will only get in the way. So it is better if they are not there at all because you can't keep bringing them in just because a war breaks out.

Those people who think like that have the last word in the sense that there is some unfairness in the way women are treated in the Armed Forces as opposed to men. For example, it is said that women shouldn't complain about not getting the top jobs because there are fewer of them and they cannot expect to. But they don't mention that for the top jobs you need combat experience so if you don't allow them to fight how can they get the top jobs? This essay is going to give special attention to that factor since it's a very big issue in the debate. (268 words)

(B) *Rewrite this conclusion to the same essay. How the redefining of 'combatant' affects the status of women is not too clear. The sentences need to be arranged in a better order. Reduce to about 90 words.*

The above makes clear that women in the armed forces are not as equal as they should be. Things change all the time but it is difficult to foresee the future and how things might change for women. For example, the question of combatant or non-combatant. More and more killing is done by remote control. According to the Geneva Convention all military personnel, including nurses, are really combatant in their eyes, regardless of sex. So who is combatant and who isn't? Only the civilians? But they get killed anyway, don't they? Did you know that more civilians have been killed in the wars since 1945 than soldiers? Anyway, the woman aircraft-controller who helps the pilot to destroy his target can be considered just as much a killer, in most people's eyes. Personally, I think that, although I agree that they should be just as equal, women are by nature pacifists and that might help the world to be, so I think they should be encouraged in that direction, regardless. (172 words)

CASE STUDIES

Christine's scrambled thinking

Religious Studies was not one of Christine's best subjects. When faced with such moral issues as in the essay topic:

Should charity be left to the State?

she felt her brain getting churned up and words running riot.

She made some good points. She showed that there was room in a Christian society for charities. The State could not be expected to notice every personal problem, she argued. Of course it should set an example by subsidies to charities and tax concessions, and so on. But there should be more control over the way charities were organised and over their financial arrangements, so that the money didn't end up in the wrong hands. There were people receiving charity who didn't need it; there were cases of organisers who embezzled it.

Christine's introduction: first version
She found it hard to get a grip on the introduction. She began:

> In today's complex society the lack and surplus of money and possessions in relation to the bare essentials of life is an important factor in the way we conduct ourselves towards charities and people who are less fortunate than ourselves. The dilemma is whether we feel morally obliged to the people and give up some of our less important needs that make up our comfortable lives, compared to such as the homeless living in cardboard boxes on the streets. Or is the state or themselves all that the less fortunate needs or deserves for that matter as the case may be.
>
> One of the main private helps which a person may give is to make a donation to a charity. There are over a thousand charities in the UK alone which are all mainly based upon helping those who have suffered disease or loss of a limb or mental problems. Charities also act as education to people about the difficulties of others.

Tutor's comment
The tutor had said this was letting the rest of the essay down. She said it was scrambled egg and that Christine would have to unscramble it. Christine had asked how you unscramble an egg and the tutor had said you take a new egg out of the fridge and start again.

'Read the rest of your essay carefully, then rewrite your introduction so that it makes clear how you're going to answer the question and what your view is, more or less. Remember you're dealing with religious studies. I think you should bring Christianity into it, or any other religion that has something to say about charity.'

Christine had time to leave the essay for a day or two. She then looked at it with fresh eyes.

Christine's new introduction
She rewrote:

> It is easier to give to charity if you are rich, but is there a moral obligation? If you are a Christian you will remember that Christ said it was harder for a rich man to get into heaven than a camel through the eye

of a needle. Many rich people feel guilty and giving to one or two charities makes them feel better. Poor people remember the story of the Good Samaritan, and give because they consider it is a Christian duty. Others, both rich and poor, argue that the Welfare State was set up to make sure that all unfortunate people who needed extra help through life would get it.

It is widely believed that the Government through the Welfare State should do more for charities and control them so that waste and misdirection are dealt with. It would be worth raising taxes to do it. Then indirectly most people in the country would be giving to charities.

I'm in favour of both in a way. I don't think it can be left entirely to the State, which cannot notice everything that goes wrong with people, and I will give examples of such misfortunes that have to be left to other people to help with. On the other hand, I will show in what ways the State should take more responsibility than it does now.

David's need to connect his conclusion
David was strongly in agreement with the proposition contained in:

Do you agree that capital punishment should be restored for premeditated murder?

The body of his essay took the arguments against one by one and answered them with what he believed were strong counter-arguments. For example, he set the argument that it turned society, as represented by the executioner, into a murderer against the argument that it protected society against such murderers. By killing a very few people, probably hundreds of citizens' lives were saved. Against the argument that capital punishment makes a mockery of efforts to reform criminals, is an admission of defeat, he set the argument that reform had to go along with punishment, human nature being what it is. He had other serviceable arguments. His conclusion ran:

Although those against restoring capital punishment have some arguments worth thinking about, I believe they are not strong enough to defeat the arguments in favour of its restoration. Take terrorists, for example. They kill indiscriminately, including women and children. What's the point of giving them life sentences in this case? There won't be enough prisons to contain them because terrorism is always with us and is increasing. The only thing a terrorist understands is: an eye for an eye and a tooth for a tooth, because that is the way their minds work. What applies to terrorists also applies to most other people who commit premeditated murders.

Tutor's comment
His tutor found several weaknesses in David's conclusion:

1. It did not connect with the body, but took up with the special case of terrorists. The sentence claiming to connect these with other premeditated murders was not convincing. Terrorism should have been covered in the body as an example among others. Such crimes, it should have been explained, had to be given special consideration, because they were political.
2. The conclusion should have homed in on a clinching argument that would have summed up what the separate arguments of the body amounted to.
3. The last sentence was not backed up by any evidence. The tutor felt that many premeditated murders had nothing to do with revenge, if often much to do with insanity.
4. Number 3 reveals the problem about defining 'premeditated'. David should have given his definition early in the essay, and the conclusion would need to relate that term to the final verdict.

David sat down to rewrite the conclusion.

Ann's weak finish
Ann had just finished her second draft of:

How racist are the professions?

She greatly improved her introduction by suggesting that greater solidarity among blacks as a political force was necessary at the point of entering professions, whereas there was much to be said for playing down solidarity tendencies and showing their individual capacities for integration into society during their earlier years.

The body followed her friends' suggestions; it analysed the way three professions, Politics, Law and Medicine (roughly poor to reasonable records of accommodating blacks), handle their recruitment and training. The chances for promotion in these three representative professions were compared. There was a telling case study for each profession.

Ann's conclusion
Her conclusion was:

> Too often it is not how skilful or how qualified you are that is the criterion, but the colour of your skin. There is both direct and indirect discrimination. Direct discrimination means treating people differently because of the colour of their skin. Indirect discrimination means applying a requirement or condition which may be described as equal in a formal sense as between racial groups but discriminatory in its effects. For example, to require a high standard of English for a labouring vacancy might be considered unlawful if this requirement excluded a black person who would otherwise do the job well. The same kinds of discrimination probably apply in the professions.

Tutor's comment
Anne was reasonably satisfied now with the first two parts of the essay, but a satisfactory conclusion was eluding her. The first sentence was strong, but she needed to show briefly how it had been supported by the evidence in the essay. From there the essay melted away. The points about the two kinds of discrimination had already been made, and this was no more than repeating them. A strong point was needed to finish. She began to rewrite the conclusion. She was nearly there.

SUMMARY

Introductions and conclusions give the most noticeable signs of your personal mark on the subject. Introductions should persuade readers that what you have to say is worth close attention. Conclusions should indicate that your contribution is worth remembering.

- **Introductions** should make it clear that the essay will attempt to satisfy the specific requirements of the title and the general requirements of the tutor. There should be control but not over-confidence. The way ahead may be shown as in a map or as in the blueprint for a building. Terms may have to be defined, issues clarified, and background described. The explanation and argument to follow can then be clearly understood. Interest in the subject should be zealously aroused.
- **Conclusions** must show that the body of evidence adds up to the viewpoint or verdict stated. The conclusion should show that a creditable attempt has been made to satisfy the requirements of topic and tutor. It should be interesting and memorable and will often stimulate readers to continue thinking about the subject.

9

Improving Your Style

Q. When he went, had you gone, and had she, if she wanted to and were able, for the time being excluding all the restraints on her not to go also, would he have brought you, meaning you and she, with him to the station?

A. Mr Brooks: Objection. That question should be taken out and shot.

From a US court case, quoted in Richard Lederer, *Anguished English*. Robson Books Ltd, 1987.

We have covered three of the four elements of PROCESS, and now it is time for the final one, Style. Chapter 6 discussed the writing techniques required for the structural patterns that different essay topics require. This chapter moves in closer, to scrutinise the brushstrokes — the words and the sentences.

WHAT IS STYLE?

Style is inseparable from the content of what you have to say, not something you clothe it with. It is inseparable from yourself, too, not something you can suddenly acquire. First decide what are the most compelling things you have to say about the topic. Style is then saying them as effectively as possible, in the way that comes naturally to you.

Your style will vary in different pieces of writing, depending on the purpose and the audience, but *you* should be there throughout these changes. You will aim to improve your style too, but much of the improvement will come unconsciously. Style is not to be improved by forcing into it an effect that doesn't naturally belong. What you can do is look at it closely, knowing what you are looking for, make a note of what would be better, and work towards that in your own way.

This chapter will help you to do that. It will help you to:

* be simple and direct
* be clear and precise

- add concrete to abstract
- take care with jargon
- develop your tone of voice
- put power into your sentences.

BE SIMPLE AND DIRECT

These two words sum up all the principles of good writing. Like all other suggestions in this book, they must be adapted to your purposes and personality.

Once you have something to say, concentrate on expressing it, in your writing, as near as you can to the simple and direct language you would use if speaking. Do not try to impress the audience with your knowledge and your thoughts. Concentrate on making what you have to say first **relevant** to the topic, then **interesting** and **readable**. This often means rewriting more than once. On the whole, the easier something is to read, the harder it was to write.

Use short words where you can

This principle is sometimes expressed as:

- short words rather than long ones
- Anglo-Saxon words rather than Romance ones (Latin origin)
- familiar words rather than unfamiliar ones whenever possible.

Sometimes, of course, the long or Romance word is the best for the purpose.

hard	or	inflexible?
tell	or	communicate?
kill	or	annihilate?
kind	or	benevolent?

Using the down-to-earth, physical, one-syllable Anglo-Saxon words among the more subtle, generalised Romance ones will make for clarity and conciseness.

Use familiar words where possible

Here are some examples of *familiar words* that are often more suitable than their less familiar (or just longer) synonyms:

choice	alternative
buy	purchase
inform	apprise
enough	sufficient
live	reside
only	exclusively
help	facilitate
show	evince
if	provided that

Is it necessary to call a diplomatic row 'the projection of a long-standing difference of emphasis'?

Avoid 'empty' words

Such conjunctions as 'whereas' and 'whereby' should be avoided. So should the circumlocutions in prepositional phrases such as:

in connection with	with
in respect of	of
for the reason that	because

Prune adjectives and adverbs

Adjectives and adverbs should be pruned ruthlessly from first drafts. These include gushing ones — 'fabulous', 'tremendous' (adjectives), and 'extremely' and 'terribly' (adverbs). The superlative degree, and near-superlatives, must earn their place, and rarely do: adjectives 'all', 'none', 'perfect'; and adverbs 'totally', 'always', 'never', 'completely', 'wholly' are examples.

We all have our favourite words of praise that slip through our guards when a more suitable and more precise word is required. One of mine is 'effective', and you may spot others in the course of reading this book. Beware of: 'powerful', 'significant', 'important', 'magnificent', 'potent', 'cogent', 'compelling', 'real', 'striking'. They are often added unnecessarily to a specific reference to some merit, especially in Literature essays.

Avoid adjectives that are 'ready and willing' to come in pairs when one is enough. It is too easy to put alliterative ones like 'mean and moody' together.

'Very ill' is all right, but 'very great' only shows your lack of confidence in 'great'. 'Inevitably' and 'predictably' at the start of a sentence are used to suggest more thought than is there.

Using adjectives for compression

Well chosen adjectives (particularly) and adverbs can be used for compression. In an essay on Joseph Conrad's novel *The Secret Agent* Francis
King says:

> The story, with its intricate weaving of comedy and suspense,
> becomes yet more ominous from the wonderful way in which Conrad
> evokes the murky squalor of London at the turn of the century: the
> crooked alleyways, the smoke-wreathed cafes; the flaring gas-jets;
> the cabs drawn by emaciated horses; the pervasive grime and fog and
> gloom.

Both the adjectives that assess the work (ominous, intricate) and the
other, purely descriptive ones, are clearly pulling their weight. The
reviewing columns of the quality papers, which need to sum up the
qualities of a film or play briefly, are good models for this kind of
compression.

Avoid ready-made phrases

They are used to suggest stronger links than are there, or to add thought-
fulness. They include, 'I am inclined to think that . . .', 'it is significant
that . . .' and, worse, such double negatives as 'it would certainly not be
unrewarding to consider . . .' On the other hand, the occasional chatty
aside ('if the truth must be told') that are common in speech can
lubricate and give the reader time to take breath.

BE CLEAR AND CONCISE

Handling facts and figures

Clarity in many essays depends on gathering the facts, figures and quotations needed for evidence and then using them to make specific points.
'A great deal of unemployment in the first three months of the year,
more than the same period last year' is vague: 'a 2.9 million average
unemployment figure for the first three months, an increase of 8 per cent
. . .' is probably what is wanted.

Similarly, lengthy praise of an author in a Literature essay, using such
abstractions as 'impressive' and 'lyrical', will not convince without specific reference to work.

Clarity means accuracy in the figures and facts presented, correct
spellings of words, especially names. If there are errors in these, your
reader will not have confidence in anything you write.

Use precise language

It is the precision of the language that is the most noticeable quality of good writing. Not the most obvious word, you feel, but the inevitable one. When Ernest Hemingway was asked why he rewrote 37 times the last page of his novel *Farewell to Arms* — what was the problem? — he said, 'Getting the words right'.

The problem — and the glory — is the rich vocabulary of English, with words collected from many other languages. It is easy to make the wrong choices. 'Chronic' is not the same as 'acute', and the following are often confused:

alternatives	choices
anticipate	expect
judicious	judicial
continuous	continual
oblivious to	ignorant of
replica	reproduction
infer	imply

Use verbs for vigour

'A negative attitude to the proposal was expressed by the government' is improved by the more direct 'The government expressed a negative attitude . . .' Use the active voice rather than the passive whenever you can.

Even better is 'The government rejected the proposal'. The meaning goes into the verb instead of being diffused among the colourless 'expressed', 'negative', 'attitude': this sort of diffusion produces bland, boring prose. You might object that 'reject' is too strong. 'Disapproved of' may not be quite strong enough. If the right word doesn't come readily, try using a thesaurus.

Notice, however, that the **analysing** and **arguing** tasks of an essay need abstract language that is objective rather than subjective, intellectual rather than emotional. The passive forms of the verb are therefore used more often than in other kinds of writing in cautious, impersonal constructions such as:

It may be assumed that . . .
It was to the credit of . . .

If they become a habit, remove some.

CONCRETE EXPRESSIONS AND ABSTRACT IDEAS

Intersperse the needed abstractions of academic essays with concrete language, as do the best non-fiction, journalism or books. The way such prose uses anecdotes and other concrete language reflects the simplicity and vigour of Christ's parables. Open any page of the Bible and you will be struck by the pictorial force of the language:

> Consider the ravens, for they sow not, neither do they reap, neither have they storehouse nor barn, and God feedeth them. How much are you more valuable than they? (*Luke, XII, 24*).

The writer of an Economics essay today might be tempted more windily to say:

> The excessive preoccupation with the accumulation of wealth betrays a reluctance in mankind to deposit the same amount of trust in Providence as is deposited by birds. Human beings should be appreciative of the fact that birds are provided with the necessities of life despite the fact that they show no such preoccupation.

Using abstract language holds a particular danger — that readers are free to make their own interpretations, their own pictures. That is why it is so important to **define your terms**. Can your definition be concrete, pictorial? — so much the better. By sending out a picture as near as possible to the meaning you want to express, you prevent readers from making up their own pictures too far from your meaning.

Being concrete, of course, may mean recourse to the other four senses as well. In an essay on pollution, for example, it may be useful to take readers into a polluted river to experience with all their senses the poison and decay as well as to present them with arguments in the abstract.

Where your language has to be mainly abstract, it does not have to be dull, as is proved by the best of the quality papers' leaders and political commentaries, and by the best-written non-fiction books.

Abstract nouns to avoid

Among abstract nouns to avoid (as well as 'attitude') are:

basis
condition

character
nature
problem
question
proposition

For 'the nature of our planning is on a long-term basis', just say 'our planning is long-term'. And so on.

HANDLING JARGON

There is good jargon — the necessary technical terms of a subject/ profession — and bad jargon, for which there are many uncomplimentary synonyms and near-synonyms. Bad jargon can be dismissed as balderdash, bunkum, drivel, gibberish, rigmarole and gobbledygook.

Using technical terms

Let's consider first the technical jargon, the special terms or slang that you might need in different disciplines. For example, if you are writing a Law essay, you could be expected to understand and use such terms as 'plaintiff', 'plead', 'damages', 'contempt' (of court), 'serious prejudice', 'defamation', 'malicious falsehood', 'qualified privilege', and so on.

When to define
Unless specifically asked for definitions you would use such terms without defining them in your Law essay. When using the terms in another discipline you would often have to define them, especially those words that have also a general meaning which is different: 'plead', 'damages', 'contempt', 'prejudice' and 'privilege' for example. In Psychology 'response' and 'stimulation' have special jargon meanings, in Chemistry there is 'effervesce', and so on.

When key terms in a discipline are constantly being reassessed — such as 'sanity' and 'insanity' in Psychology — you must be constantly vigilant. Seek guidance from your tutor when necessary. Terms whose connotations vary from discipline to discipline must be watched: consider how the word 'natural' varies in this way. Not only that: consider how its meaning changes from one period to the next, along with the current ways of looking at the world, when you are studying Literature or History for example.

There is much jargon in Literature studies. Such terms as 'Classic' and 'Romantic' for periods; 'classic' and 'romantic' for styles, 'romantic

novel', 'science fiction', 'mystery' and 'thriller' for genres may sometimes need to be defined — or at least any special attitude of your own
to them explained. Moreover, 'tragic' as a genre term has to be distin-
guished from the everyday meaning of 'disastrous'.

Unacceptable jargon

Gibberish we can usually avoid, but gobbledygook — the jargon of
bureaucracy — is a disease that spreads if not ruthlessly cut back. It con-
fuses while it purports to make clear. It usually appears in the form of
overlong and overcomplicated sentences. The main culprits are
government departments, business organisations of all kinds, insurance
companies and banks.

Examples
Examples of gobbledygook are such phrases as:

> will be rendered inoperable
> deteriorated to a greater extent than had been envisaged
> emanated from no less than an authority than
> in view of the foregoing circumstances
> pending clarification of your current status

Can you express these statements more simply? In 1979 the Plain
English Campaign was established to persuade users of gobbledygook to
aim at clear English. It has had some success.

Clichés, euphemisms and circumlocutions
Reducing the clichés
Jargon used to the purpose, in its appropriate place, is respectable: it
becomes unrespectable when it spreads. In unsuitable places, technical
terms simply become clichés:

> interface
> user-friendly
> parameters
> the bottom line

Some are recognised as impostors and are relegated to a sort of limbo
after a year or two: 'caring', 'trendy'. Others hang around and become
so familiar that we feel it would be bad manners to complain too loudly:
'phenomenon', 'basically'.

Seeing through euphemisms
Politicians have a jargon of euphemisms to make things sound less sinister than they are:

pacification (crushing by force)
ethnic cleansing (racial murder)

and so on. In certain circles when an official body is 'not comfortable' with a situation it means it wishes its crime had not been discovered. Perhaps it had been 'economical with the truth'.

Cutting out circumlocutions
These are rife outside as well as inside gobbledygook. Some are long-standing and get by in speech but should be cut out of writing:

in a nutshell
loud and clear
mine of information

Others should be boycotted:

at this point in time
the calm before the storm
painted a grim picture

Moderate use
Figures of speech that were once vivid have become clichés. You may be aiming to avoid producing an essay that is as 'dry as dust' but you are risking 'the kiss of death' if you trot these phrases out, together with 'as loyal as an apostle', and 'as gentle as a dove'. On the other hand, you may occasionally be able to add a flash of wit by creating a fresh one.

Clichés in moderation have their uses. With their familiarity they can help to break the ice, reassure and make it easier to say goodbye. They can give the reader a breather when much else in your essay is deeper than the everyday.

But these functions are more the concern of the journalist than the essay writer, who must err on the conservative side of 'good taste'. When you feel 'uncomfortable' with a current slang or 'buzz' word, you should not use it, except occasionally in quotes. Make sure they haven't already turned too stale to use, even in quotes. At the time of writing many people are going around putting every second word into quotes with their fingers in the air. To be patronising about clichés can become the worst cliché of all.

DEVELOPING YOUR OWN TONE OF VOICE

'Tone of voice' in writing means:

- praising or blaming
- agreeing or angry
- being rough or gentle
- being kind or cruel
- applauding or hectoring.

It includes using smiles or frowns, acceptance and rejection. It must come naturally to you, as must your style as a whole. Anything fake or pretentious will spoil your chances of winning the reader over to your attitude or point of view.

There is a tone of voice suitable for essays, suitable for the purpose and the audience. The audience is, chiefly, the tutor who is going to grade it, so the essay will be formal rather than informal, serious rather than light-hearted, impersonal rather than personal. You are present everywhere and visible hardly anywhere (except when asked to be, in creative essays). Do not, however, play *too* safe, inhibited by the thought of a fault-picking judge. The judge wants an essay that is not only correct, but is also as fresh, interesting, readable, and original as the topic allows you to be.

A lecturer may be saying all the right things in the correct proportions, but if the voice is toneless, the audience will give up listening. In the same way flat, toneless writing will deter the reader. You must work at your style until every sentence needs to be read once only to be understood — and enjoyed.

What gives writing its particular tone is, in the end, a mystery, because it is inseparable from the mystery at the heart of the writer. Let it develop unconsciously, although there is no harm in experimenting (especially in your youth) by writing in the style of the writers you admire. Read good contemporary writers of fiction and poetry as well as non-fiction, so that you unconsciously pick up good rhythms.

PUTTING POWER INTO YOUR SENTENCES

Here are six rules for making simple, direct and powerful sentences:

1.   Average 15 to 20 words a sentence.
Make one main point only, restricting subsidiary points to one. The sub-heading to this paragraph is a usefully punchy beginning (seven words). Sentences much longer than 20 words are written of course: they are often, however, several sentences in one; they may, like this one, be divided by semi-colons that might just as well be full stops; they are put together to avoid having too many short sentences in sequence; but the arrangement, quite common a hundred years ago, is not too common now. (71 words)

2.   Give your sentences varied lengths, structures and rhythms.
The modern short, economical sentence can become musclebound, though. Replacing subsidiary clauses by short phrases may result in mis-leading or confusing connections:

> A loyal supporter in his youth of Tottenham Hotspur football club, the MP for Togglesworth has ambitions to become a Cabinet minister.

Over-reliance on the short, loose sentence (two clauses, the second introduced by a conjunction or relative pronoun) produces monotony, especially when the lazy 'which' reappears:

> Large hospitals which used to house the mentally ill, are empty. Many of these hospitals, which fell into decay, were demolished. Housing estates have been built on the land which was made available.

Short sentences must be interspersed with a few long ones for the sake of variety and rhythm. When a long sentence gets out of control, however, ask yourself what is the **subject**? What do I want to say about it (what is the **predicate**)? Then either reduce the sentence into clarity or divide it into two or more sentences, as has been shown at various points in this book.

3.   Use the active rather than the passive mood of the verb.
When the subject is known, 'vandals uprooted trees' is usually better than 'the trees were uprooted by vandals'.

4.   Give the result rather than the process.
'He went' is probably enough for: 'He wondered whether he should go or not, and decided that he would go, so he went'.

5. *Be positive rather than negative.*
'He failed' rather than 'he did not succeed'.

6. *Keep related words together.*
'There was a large supermarket in the town that was on the outskirts' is better expressed as '. . . supermarket on the outskirts of the town'.

Shifting your emphasis

Too many sentences of similar structure? — then rewrite some to vary the rhythm with shifts of emphasis. Here are examples of such rewriting, starting with the most common order of subject, verb, predicate:

1. Too much study and too little exercise can damage students' health and reduce their powers of concentration.

2. Damage to students' health and a reduction in powers of concentration: these are the penalties for too much study and too little exercise.

3. The penalties for too much study and too little exercise are . . .

4. It is damage to students' health . . . that too often result from . . .

5. Health damaged. Powers of concentration reduced. These are . . .

6. Not only damage to students' health but . . . can result from . . .

7. Not only does too much study and too little exercise damage . . . but they also . . .

8. Students' health can be damaged by . . . and their powers . . .

TASK

Rewrite simply and directly the following extracts in 30 minutes: (a) and (b) are gobbledygook, (c) and (d) are extracts from essays.

(a) Notice beside a lift door: 'LIFT EMERGENCIES. In the event of the lift alarm bell ringing or it is apparent that someone is trapped in the lift, please report the emergency to the Council offices by telephoning . . .'

(b) 'Your enquiry about the possibility of making use of the club notice board for the purpose of exhibiting promotional material in the form of a leaflet concerning the establishment of an Amateur Dramatic Society raises the question of the provenance and authoritativeness of the said material and whether the proposed location for it is as desirable as one would have wished.'

(c) 'The following rebellions to take place were those in Cornwall and Norfolk during Edward VIII's reign. Edward was a very weak and sickly child who therefore was not entirely able to rule on his own so had to have a Regent to help him and basically do his work for him.'

(d) *Extract from an essay on 'How far is Willy Loman responsible for the accumulating unhappiness explored in the course of the play* Death of a Salesman?':

Willy Loman, the travelling salesman, is the central character, Arthur Miller, the writer, is therefore able to make evident to the audience Willy's character flaws. Willy is inattentive, inconsistent and delusive. Which clearly doesn't suit the kind of work he's supposed to do. It is deducible that Willy's character traits are the main reasons for the accumulating unhappiness explored in the course of the play; his behaviour pattern declined to such an extent that from a critical point of view it is amazing how no one throughout the play considered him to be suffering from a medical condition such as senility — which is suggested in Act 1, even though of course they are upset by his behaviour at various times. Most of the other characters don't really sympathise with him except his wife who says, 'Attention must be paid to such a man'. He thought he was doing the best for his two sons but he brought them up to believe he was successful and they could be successful too. Anybody could be successful, all they had to do was believe in the American Dream, which was that America gave everybody the chance to be successful, you didn't have to start at the top, all you had to be was self-confident. He deluded himself and he deluded his family, but when they found out he was deceiving them about his success they lacked sympathy over his breakdown and blamed him for their own unhappiness, except as I said his wife. (251 words)

(Reduce by about a half. Make two paragraphs. If you know the play, don't be tempted to add any points. Stick to the points of the essay writer, and concentrate on presenting them as clearly as possible.)

CASE STUDIES

Neil gets his thoughts into a better order

Neil has completed an essay for GCSE Psychology on:

> Special school or mainstream school — which is the best for the child with Special Education Needs who has language and communication problems?

His tutor is quite pleased with it. 'You've summarised well the relevant authorities. So we've got Piaget on the child needing language for socialisation, Bruner on language in intellectual growth, Vygotsky saying language is for the person to be wanted and understood as part of a community, Chomsky on interactive social experience needed for language to develop.

'But this paragraph on the disadvantages of the special school needs to be ordered better. Could you rewrite it, please? The two bits about the journey should go together. Take a seven-year-old girl as your example throughout, you'll find that will help. Say "she", not "you". Be more concise.'

This was the paragraph:

> The trouble about special schools is that taking the example of a seven-year-old you don't get so much chance to talk to people as for example if you are a girl at the Brownies or if you are a boy at the Cubs. Well, you might but you're probably too tired because of the long journey. Also you wouldn't be going to shops where there is always a chance to talk to other people. Another thing about the special schools is that you usually have a long journey to get there as I've already mentioned and a child would get home very late in the evening and not in the mood being too tired to talk to anybody. Furthermore, at a special school the other children can't talk to you since they have their own language problems. (138 words)

Neil had three attempts at rewriting until he was satisfied:

> At a special school the seven-year-old SEN girl is likely to be in a class with children with similar language problems. She may not have much opportunity for stimulating conversation apart from with teachers. There might also be the disadvantage of long isolated journeys: the child would get home too late or too tired for Brownies,

shopping or other social activities. Thus opportunities for language acquisition would be reduced. (72 words)

Marjorie works on her connections and sources

In an essay on:

What are the commercial influences on media organisation?

Marjorie had a paragraph on the influence of advertisers on the British working class, radical press in the 19th century:

Starting a radical newspaper with a working class audience was cheap in those days. People volunteered to distribute, and machinery and labour was cheap. Advertising revenue was not needed. The profits came from sales and those profits covered the costs. Advertisers didn't want only working class audiences and the papers had to find other readers. Also advertisers actually refused to become clients of radical newspapers which preached anti-capitalism, and some of them were forced to close down for this reason.

It didn't quite hang together. The notes were all right, and the facts were all right, but where were the connections? Which was more important or more common: the need to get other readers, or the advertisers refusing custom? How did the advertisers suddenly appear on the scene? Also she ought to acknowledge the source.

The re-write
She wrote:

There is a convincing argument by Curran (1977) that the radical press was put out of action by the growth of advertising in the 19th century. Before that growth radical newspapers could easily cover the costs of production from sales. Production was cheap, because the machines and the labour were cheap, and the distribution was done by volunteers.

All this changed as advertisers became increasingly influential. Firstly, they were able to force papers that preached anti-capitalism to close down by refusing to give them business. Secondly, and more important, the papers were compelled to aim at a wider readership. That of course meant that the content had to become less radical.

Walter unblocks his responses

'It seems to me natural that I slip into the past tense when writing an essay about a novel. I mean the author finished writing it some years ago, and I've finished reading it. And since the whole thing is imaginary anyway . . . not only are they dead they've never been alive . . .'

Mr Ogilvie, the tutor, enjoyed the challenge that a conversation with Walter presented. 'We use the present tense because they're still alive. Every time someone opens the book they become alive for the reader. They seem more alive than real people, and we can respond to them as we read.'

Walter was not quite convinced.

'With other subjects I haven't got the problem of response. There are so many facts to respond to.'

'In Literature your material is emotions, feelings, imaginary events. But these are just as much *facts* as the normal non-fiction kind, aren't they? Responding means recognising the value of these sorts of facts and your language should reflect this recognition or respect. By the way I saw that respect creeping into your last essay, despite what you say.'

'You know, I'm beginning to see the light.'

SUMMARY

Your writing style means *how* you say what you have to say, keeping in mind the purpose and the audience. You can improve your style both unconsciously and consciously.

- Unconscious improvement of your style is achieved by reading good writing and picking up good habits and rhythms from it.

- Conscious improvement of your style is achieved by noting the weaknesses you and your readers find in it, and by trying to follow the principles those weaknesses disregard. The principles of good style can be summed up as:

  1. Be as simple and direct as possible. Aim to *express* your ideas rather than impress with them. Use short, familiar words when you can.

  2. Be clear and precise, in facts and figures as well as in language. Make verbs and nouns carry your meaning, rather than adjectives and adverbs.

3. Use concrete nouns rather than abstract. Essays often need abstract language, so intersperse it with concrete examples, even the occasional figure of speech, to enliven the style.

4. Use necessary jargon of the discipline with care, defining when necessary. Avoid the various kinds of unacceptable jargon — gobbledygook, clichés, slang and circumlocutions.

5. Develop your tone of voice: it must be natural and unpretentious, but for essays, on the whole, serious and impersonal without lacking freshness and readability.

6. Produce powerful sentences. They should average 15 to 20 words, and be varied in lengths, structures and rhythms. Practise different ways of shifting the emphasis.

A good style is not achieved by mechanically following principles. To improve your style, make the principles work for you.

10

Editing and Rewriting

'The best judge of a feast is the guest, not the cook.' Aristotle

There are writers – and there are editors, in journalism, publishing and other businesses. Writers and editors need and respect each other. Writing is the more creative part, editing the more critical. For most writers, editing means **reducing** and some **rewriting**.

While rewriting you may also be:

- correcting
- improving
- clarifying
- adding
- reorganising
- polishing

Some editing goes on while you are writing the first draft of course, especially if you work on a word processor. The two activities merge. But writer and editor are convenient labels.

As an essay writer, *use yourself as editor* at every stage, but make use also of the editing skills of fellow-students and tutors. What this chapter aims to do is show you what editors (yourself included) look for in a draft, what they find, what they suggest, and how you can follow up those suggestions. This editing process will cover the following stages:

- **getting feedback**
- **vetting your content and flow**
- **vetting your structure**
- **vetting the style**
- **learning from criticism**

A detailed analysis of an essay will follow.

GETTING FEEDBACK

Identifying weaknesses

Get feedback in optimistic mood, from yourself and others. If you are aware of the weaknesses of the first draft, that can be considered an advantage. Are the weaknesses obvious to you? — you will be able to do something about them. Can't you see any weaknesses? — you may have to do some extra soul-searching. Have you papered over the cracks with a polished style? Do your critical faculties need developing?

Getting a fresh reaction

Whether you feel substantial revision is needed or not, put your first draft away for a day or two so that you will be able to see it with fresh eyes. At the same time make a copy or two to leave with fellow-students; ask them to produce comments at the time you have decided to rewrite.

Tutors sometimes make photocopies of students' essays and pass them round the class (if the class is not too large); each student can then write a paragraph of criticism on each fellow-student's essay. These paragraphs are collected and distributed. Then each student can comment on the criticisms received.

If this feedback activity is done at first draft stage, students will gain great benefit from being criticised and from the opportunity to develop their critical faculties on others' work. It is easier of course to see the faults in others' work than in your own.

Passing final versions round in this way is especially useful if they are on the same topic. You tend to view your final version on a topic as the only possible arrangement. Seeing several other arrangements at this stage opens your eyes to the variety of ways a topic can be treated.

All editing should be done cautiously.

- Use a pencil and an eraser if you are editing a typescript, so that second and third thoughts don't turn into a battlefield of scribbles.

- First check that the essay is of the correct length.

- Then read through the draft three times, looking for different things: first for content and flow, second for structure, third for style.

VETTING YOUR CONTENT AND FLOW

Overall shape

Reading the draft for content and flow, first consider the overall shape:

- Is the flow maintained in unity and coherence?

- Is the topic dealt with adequately?

- Is the purpose of the essay clear?

- Has it been fulfilled?

Are there smooth transitions?

Are you kept on course by smooth transitions — links that take you from sentence to sentence, paragraph to paragraph without jerky changes of gear? Do these links include key words and phrases related to the key words of the title? In this first reading, don't stop to worry about details, though, or you won't see the wood for the trees. Underline in pencil where you will want to scrutinise and improve at rewriting stage.

Deletions and insertions

Bracket off in pencil any possible deletions. Indicate any possible insertions where there is a step missing in an argument or a gap in an explanation, or patches of vagueness.

Leave the detailed consideration of word power till reading 3, but underline any dubious words or phrases as you go — for example, confusing changes of subject, alterations in the point of view or approach, inconsistencies in style that irritate (not the same thing as the variety that helps to make a piece readable).

Underline anything in the following checklist that may not be satisfactory.

Checklist for vetting content

- Are all important **aspects** of the topic covered?

- Is there a topic sentence indicating the one aspect covered by each paragraph, or is it clear anyway what that aspect is?

- Are all paragraphs, sentences, facts, points, made **relevant** to the topic of the essay?

- Are all *main* points/opinions backed up by some kind of **evidence** — proof, examples, convincing arguments?

- Has the content been **selected** to give the right **emphasis**?

- Would the points/arguments convince if the topic were opened up to **discussion**? (Your feedback should indicate whether they would.)

- Are sources acknowledged?

Troubleshooting decisions
Before the second draft, you may need to overhaul the content.

1. More reading or re-reading or other research, with note-taking, may be required if, for example, there is a lack of evidence or too many irrelevancies. Irrelevancies suggest that you have not evaluated carefully enough what you have read.

2. More thinking and planning may be required if there are gaps in the train of thought, or confused sections. See if you can relate such gaps and confusions to parts of the plan. If the fault is in the plan, correct it. The plan may need to be redone. (See next vetting section.)

VETTING YOUR STRUCTURE

Your second reading is to vet the structure. You should have a checklist to follow already — in your plan. Do you have only a sketchy plan, or no plan at all? Then make a plan that follows exactly the essay you have (as is done below to illustrate the analysis of an essay), so that any weaknesses will be revealed. Check that the points made by each paragraph follow a logical pattern. Let's take, for example, an essay on:

Which activities of the United Nations have been described as setting standards for member states and which of these activities have provided the most impressive examples?

Separate paragraphs might deal with:

1. The UN's promotion of human rights.

2. The emphasis on the need for clean drinking water globally.

3. The pressure on South Africa to end apartheid rule.

4. The nuclear non-proliferation treaty.

5. The efforts on behalf of refugees.

6. The attacks on racial discrimination.

TASK 1

Put these points in a better order, justifying your arrangement, and then compare with the suggested response in Appendix A.

Within expository paragraphs you are likely to put main points first, followed by subsidiary points, in most important to least important order, as in the concluding paragraph to the Armed Forces essay on page 115. Note that the first, topic sentence of this paragraph includes the whole: each subsequent sentence becomes increasingly specific.

Improving your links

Much has been said about links. At the editing stage look for links that you can improve. Especially watch out for cliché links that don't express precisely enough what the connection is with what went before.

'Additionally' and 'however' are familiar culprits here. The first is often used when what follows is more than merely another point. 'However' often suggests a contrast with what went before when it *is* just another point.

Some of the cliché links can be replaced by other techniques mentioned in Chapter 5, notably by skilful stitching in of key words and phrases. Make sure, however, that there are not too many synonyms and that there is some repetition of the exact word or phrase throughout the essay.

Linking can often be done subtly without making the reader over-conscious of it. An idea is developed, for example, by recasting it in different words.

Example

Consider the following pair of sentences from an essay on 'How important is the role of the mass media and education in producing conformity and consensus?' (Open University):

> So it seems that there may be quite a lot of consistency in the dominant ideas and values presented by both the media and the education system. There is still, however, the question of whether people tend to absorb these messages or whether they form their view of society more objectively.

'Dominant ideas and values' are neatly encapsulated by 'messages'.

Parallelism in paragraphs and sentences

If one paragraph is about night and the next about day, 'parallelism' will make their roles in the total structure immediately clear. The first paragraph might run: 'At night . . . in the middle of the night . . . at the break of dawn . . .' The second might run: 'In the early morning . . . midday . . . by late evening . . .' Such a pattern can obviously be repeated when organising according to the logic of space or from general to specifics.

Sentences have their parallelisms, too. This sentence, though quite simple, is not as clear as it might be:

> The MP had never travelled by car to nearby Chichester alone, much less a meeting in London.

The grammar suggests either that the meeting might be travelling to London too, or that the meeting is somehow being compared with 'alone'. The word 'alone' is out of place.

Rewrite:

> The MP had never travelled alone by car even to nearby Chichester, much less to a meeting in London.

Shifting 'alone' and balancing 'even to' in the first part with 'much less to' in the second part make the two parts of the sentence parallel — and clearer. 'Never travelled alone' clearly relates to the two destinations.

VETTING YOUR STYLE

At this stage of the editing — let's say the third reading — see that there is sufficient variety in lengths and shapes of sentences and words, and that the emphases are in the right places. (Stylistic matters concerning the whole essay and paragraphs have been dealt with under structure.) Scrutinise any sentences and words that you have underlined during your first reading because they didn't look right. Now work at putting them right.

Make a note, if you haven't done so already, of the faults of style covered in Chapter 9 that you are prone to, and look especially for these in the essay you are editing.

Checklist of style faults

Here is a brief checklist of some key points of style to watch:

- Are some of the **sentences too long**? (Keep to an average of around 15-20 words)

- Do all sentences contain just **one main point**?

- Is the meaning/action concentrated in **verbs** where possible, rather than in nouns?

- Are the verbs **active** wherever possible rather than passive?

- Are the **tenses** of the verbs consistent?

- Is the **tone** of voice consistent?

- Is the **order of words** in the sentences the clearest order? Are subject, verb and object as close to each other as possible?

- Is there **padding** in some of the phrases? Are there unnecessary adjectives and adverbs?

- Is there unnecessary **repetition**?

LEARNING FROM CRITICISM

The most important lesson to be learned from reading tutors' criticism is, of course **how to improve your own critical faculties**.

One way to do this is to read over tutors' comments on your past essays before you begin a new essay, and before working on final versions.

You might find it useful to list tutors' comments as they arrive, under such headings as Content, Evidence, Structure, Style, and Summing Up. You will find that the comments will focus on the following requirements:

Content:	Have you read enough?
Evidence:	Have you sufficient references, examples, cases, proofs, quotations, quotes?
Structure:	Have you departed from your plan? Is your plan faulty? Did you neglect to do a plan?
Style:	You may want to use the subheadings Paragraphs, Sentences, Phrases, Words, Tone of Voice, Consistency, Readability.
Summing up:	Most tutors give a summing up as well as picking up on details. Compare this with any other feedback you have received. If you disagree with your tutor's summing up, try to discuss it with him/her. You may find that you had not expressed certain points as clearly as you thought you had. You may find that things you thought were on paper are still in your head. You may be surprised to find that you have misinterpreted what you have read.

You may occasionally be able to persuade a tutor to revise the judgement — but of course you will succeed or fail in this magnanimously!

Examples of tutor's criticism

Consider the following samples of tutors' criticisms:

On evidence
Criticism: 'There was an extent to which some of the issues were oversimplified. Waugh's *Officers and Gentlemen*, for instance, has a far from clear-cut position on class, tradition and privilege. Yes, Waugh laments the erosion of tradition, but by the same token that tradition is weighed in the balance and found wanting in Crete. Your essay would have been stronger had there been some detailed digging into specific episodes of this kind.'

On context/argument
Text: 'Private schools . . . have to appeal to parents whose expectations
are likely to be influenced by their knowledge of state schools.'
('knowledge' underlined)
Criticism: 'Or lack of?'

On style
Text: 'Although societies inevitably have some conflict and disorder . . .'
('inevitably' underlined)
Criticism: 'Why "inevitably", I wonder?'

On summing up
Criticism: 'I feel that you could have wrestled a little more with the issue
of the relative contributions of nature and nurture to cognitive development and the implications of this to care-giving.' (Psychology)
    'I do not want to give the impression that your ideas, or the way they
are developed, are somehow wrong: it's more a case of your essay
needing, for a higher grade, more analysis and clarification and less
description.' (Literature)
    Tutors are generally as helpful and encouraging as possible in their
criticisms.

DETAILED ANALYSIS OF AN ESSAY

Study Version A of the essay, 'What is education for?', the vetting guide
and the further suggestions for rewriting it in preparation for the next
task, which will be to do the rewrite.

Version A   What is education for?

(I) The term 'education' is very wide and can encompass every
learning experience in life. To this end we talk about the
'University of Life' as a euphemism for all life's learning
experiences. Used in this form the term 'education' is too wide
5   ranging and so in this essay I will concentrate on just formal
education. We need all kinds of knowledge and skills in order to
survive. As far as the schools are concerned, we need education
that will help us get a job or follow a career as well as help us
10   to get satisfaction out of life and know how to get on with
ourselves and with each other peacefully.
(II) Human beings are unique in the animal world in that no other

animal cares for its young as long as humans do. We care for our young for about twenty years on average which perhaps explains why it is that man rules the planet. The aim of formal education

15 should be to help with this process and hence develop mature and well adjusted human beings.

(III) I'm not interested here in sociological and political theories. For example, Marxists say that education maintains the inequalities of the class system. This essay is about life as a whole and

20 the fact that education has to prepare us for it. As I said we live in a very complex world and we seem to need this length of time to be able to pass on to the next generation all the skills that are necessary to be able to flourish in this complex environment. So the aim of education should be to help

25 launch our youngsters into the world as fully developed as possible and to give them every chance of success. To this end four areas of development can be identified. We require development physically, mentally, spiritually and socially. We will now look at these areas in turn.

30 (IV) Physical development largely takes place naturally as a result of growing up but it can be assisted by careful use of physical activities. In formal education these tend to split into two distinct types of activity. We have physical education (PE) and 'games'. The ultimate aim of the two is essentially the

35 same which is to further physical development of the individual, but the emphasis is different. The former is on direct development by means of exercise whereas the latter is on indirect development by means of playing games.

(V) Nearly every area of formal education concerns itself with

40 some form of mental development. In general terms this means being able to take information in from the world, being able to process the information, being able to store the information and then being able to express what has been assimilated to others in a suitable form. For reasons of convenience, these abilities are

45 often taught as separate subjects but in reality they all merge and overlap since they are used together. So for example reading and writing are often taught as separate subjects but they are really two sides of the same coin.

(VI) The spiritual dimension of education involves a much wider

50 view than just religion or religious knowledge. It encompasses aspects of life such as honesty, integrity and moral values. It also encompasses such ideas as self worth and peace of mind. These

are not normally taught directly as such but rather they are
picked up by those in education by the standards and
55   attitudes of their teachers.
(VII) The social development of the individual covers areas such
as learning to mix well with others, learning to be assertive
rather than aggressive. Additionally it involves learning self-discipline and having an understanding of the law and authority.
60   (VIII) 'Education has for its object the formation of character,'
said the philosopher Herbert Spencer and this is a strong
component of most education. People should be able to develop
their own individual characters under guidance of course and not
be repressed before they start. You don't want everybody coming
65   out of school to have the same thoughts and the same
personalities.
(IX) Don't forget many famous people like Churchill didn't do
all that well at school. If you don't stimulate their curiosity and
they get bored, who is to blame? The worst fault of some schools
70   is that they don't succeed in stimulating curiosity, the result is
that there are too many dropouts who never recover and never do
well. If you don't have curiosity, you're unlikely to produce
anything in your life. Do we want everybody to be conventional
thinking the same way as everybody else? What does it mean to
75   think creatively? It means to decide for yourself what you think
and not just reproduce other people's opinions. I don't think you
should overdo it though. Too much individuality upsets the
balance. You don't want a nation of neurotics.
(X) We have looked at the four areas simply as a means of
80   splitting the problem of education down into more manageable
chunks. As such there are no real divisions between the areas. If
you consider playing football for example it is easy to see that
there are aspects of each area involved. The physical element is
easy to see since it involves physical activity. The mental aspect
85   is there in the form of deciding what moves to make and when.
The spiritual side is there in the form of 'team spirit' and playing
fairly. Finally football is a social game since you play as part of
a team. Similar arguments can be made for almost any activity.
90   (XI) Returning to the complexity of the modern world, change is
certainly rapid and confusing. You need to collect information
quickly. Fortunately we have the computer and television,
making 'a global village'.
(XII) Formal education then is part of the process of forming well

95   developed, mature human beings who are well equipped to thrive
       in our complex society. As such I would sum up its aims as
       creating the skeleton upon which life and the individual may later
       hang the flesh. Having been educated the individual has all the
       techniques available to him to be able to function effectively in
100   the world thus leaving the individual in a position to further
       develop and mature as they see fit.
(1,000 words approximately)

Vetting guide: the 'Process' of Version A

General

Purpose
The essay's purpose is to show that formal education helps to develop
people in four ways: physically, mentally, spiritually and socially.

Content
The four aspects are analysed and discussed separately for convenience,
and an attempt at synthesis is made towards the end. The broadest definition of education is used — the preparation for life — and sociology
and politics are avoided. The ideal result of formal education is people
mature enough to live happily and fruitfully, fulfilling their potential, at
peace with themselves and others, benefiting, in a rapidly changing
world, from the new information technology.

Structure
The four aspects of education are analysed and discussed in the order
indicated, after which they are shown operating together in football.
This helps to provide a visible structure, but the essay lacks a unifying
thread and a connected, logical argument. The essay concludes by referring to the complexity of the modern world, and indicating that on the
foundation laid by formal education individuals through their
experience of life will build.

Style
There is some good thinking reflected in straightforward language,
forceful without being hectoring, but there is a lack of linking words and
phrases, especially where they are most needed to link paragraphs. The
attempt to avoid repetition by providing several near-synonyms (see
notes on lines 51/55 below) makes for vagueness if not confusion.

Paragraph outline

I   For the purpose of this essay, the term will be narrowed down to formal education.

II   Education for humans is a long process: the formal part must help to produce mature human beings.

III   Education for life as a whole is to be discussed, not sociological or political theories of education. There are four aspects to be considered: physical, mental, spiritual, and social.

IV   Physical education at school is achieved directly (PE) and indirectly (games).

V   Mental education means developing the ability to take in information, process it, store it, assimilate it and reproduce it. This seems to mean developing study skills: learning how to read, listen, make notes, develop the memory and thinking power. These skills are often combined for particular tasks. (The analogy with a computer, though, is inadequate.)

VI   The spiritual aspect includes morality, self-esteem and serenity.

VII   The social aspect includes self-discipline and self-expression as well as consideration for others.

VIII   The formation of character and individuality must also be encouraged. (This cuts across spiritual and social aspects and suggests the limiting to four aspects is causing difficulty.)

IX   Schools don't do enough to stimulate curiosity. Creativity means thinking for yourself. Too much individuality makes you neurotic. (This paragraph is out of control. It should have been divided at 'Do we want . . .?' but with the three attributes — curiosity, creativity and individuality – connected in a clear argument.)

X   The four aspects of education are seen at work in football.

XI   The rapid pace of change in the modern world is confusing, but computers help. (Again, it's not clear how this fits in.)

XII Conclusion: Formal education aims to produce well-balanced human beings who can continue to develop through their experience of life.

Analysis

lines

1   What is the difference between 'wide' and 'very wide'? – 'can' unnecessary. Read: '. . . wide and encompases . . .'

2   'To this end' is a faked link: it is not to this end that we talk . . For 'talk about' read 'use'.

3   For 'euphemism' read 'label'.

4/5   Repetition: read 'I will therefore concentrate . . .'

5/6   'Formal education . . . schools . . .' What exactly is the scope of the essay?

11   Lack of link to paragraph II. It would be better to start with the point in the middle that the period of formal education must be long.

15   '. . . this process' appears to link up with ruling the planet, instead of with the long period of care.

17   The sentences of paragraph III are in a confusing order, and there is repetition. The paragraph should begin with the fourth sentence, since it makes a link with the previous paragraph. Delete 'as I said' and 'seem to'. The first two sentences about Marxism should be put at the end of the paragraph, but must be linked in to the discussion.

27   For 'areas of development' read 'aspects'.

30/38   This discussion of physical education doesn't lead anywhere. A more fruitful comparison would be the greater emphasis on team spirit in games. There is discussion of this in lines 73-83 so this aspect should be dealt with in one place. There should be a link between team spirit and character building (lines 49-55).

39   Even though the four aspects have been signposted and we know the next to be discussed is mental development, each paragraph should be bridged somehow to the next, and there should not be a plunge like this. It would be best to leave mental till the last since it is the key aspect, and since character building is more directly related to physical, social and spiritual.

40   The definition of mental development misses the growth of analytical and argumentative power. 'Skills' would be a better term here than 'abilities' to describe what is *taught*. Abilities are not subjects.

45/48 Overlapping of subjects should cover the whole range if it is to be mentioned at all. These lines add nothing to that aspect so should be deleted.

49   There is no link to spiritual development. 'Moral' would be a better term than 'spiritual', especially since the point is made that the discussion is not merely about religious knowledge/experience. The spiritual could be included as part of the morality aspect.

51/55 For 'aspects . . . such as . . . values' read: 'such moral values as charity and integrity' since 'honesty' is covered by 'integrity'. The chain 'aspects . . . values . . . ideas . . . standards . . . attitudes . . .' is confusing. They might all have been replaced by such a term as 'qualities' and then the argument would have been clearer.

52/55 I think 'self worth' and 'peace of mind' are better related to mental health in general than to morality, although there is a strong connection with morality. They are characteristics or qualities to be developed rather than 'ideas'.

54/55 These qualities are inculcated in various ways at school, directly and indirectly in various subjects, not merely by the good examples set by teachers, however important they may be.

56   No link to social development. The brief paragraph on this aspect is inadequate. No indication is given of how the educational system includes this aspect of learning.

60   Character building should be included in the section on moral values.

67/68   The sentence on Churchill belongs to the previous paragraph, but even there the train of thought would not be clear without his connection with individuality.

71   '. . . who never recover . . .' From what?

72/78   It is clear that this part of the essay needs rethinking.

79/81   Read: 'In the above discussion education has been divided into four aspects for convenience. We can now see how they work together.' (Education has not been seen as a problem, and 'as such' won't do as a link.) Paragraph X has another confusing chain of near-synonyms for 'aspects': 'areas', 'chunks', 'divisions', 'element' and 'side'. It is easy to keep to 'aspects' in this paragraph, with the odd 'they'. To show the aspects working together needs a survey through various subjects rather than a close look at football.

91/92   The change of subject — 'You . . . we . . .' — can be avoided.

94   '. . . then . . .' is a poor link.

96   'As such' again is a faked link.

98   The metaphor doesn't quite work. 'Hang the flesh' meaning additional development is unfortunate when talking about humans. 'A foundation on which to build' will be safer.

100   Repetition of 'individual'.

101   'they' should have followed a singular antecedent.

Criticism

The main merit of Version A is the painstaking analysis, in parts, of different aspects of formal education. The subject is so wide that there is a danger of dressing up the obvious. Essay A doesn't avoid the danger.

The title needs spelling out in some such terms as:

What do *you* think are the main purposes of education at present, and how far do you agree with the priorities?

You might be even more gimlet-eyed, and detect a hidden agenda:

We know what education is supposed to be for — to produce well balanced, moral human beings qualified to embark on a useful job and carry out their responsibilities to a future family and to the rest of society — but is it as effective as it should be in these aims, and are there aims that ought to be made more explicit? Are there some kinds of brainwashing going on, for instance?

The crucial aspect of 'mental' education is discussed as if the mind were a computer. What about teaching people to think: developing powers of analysis and logical argument? The new information technology should have been considered.

Further suggestions for rewriting

Apart from the various hints to be extracted from the commentaries above, here are some further suggestions.

Structure

The purpose of the essay is diffused in paragraphs I to III. It should be indicated more quickly and clearly. Paragraphs IV, VII and VIII in particular need to be re-thought and rewritten. The contribution of PE and games (IV) should not be separated from social aspects (VII) and character building (VIII). To make the connection between physical and mental the Latin tag *mens sana in corpore sano* (sound mind in a sound body) could be invoked.

Suggested outline for version B

(Compare with the outline for version A, pages 150–151).

I   Education defined: development of full potential. The purpose of the essay is to show what kinds of knowledge and skills in formal education prepare for fulfilling adult life.

II   The system must foster both social and individual development: these terms defined.

III The knowledge that helps in these developments passes from one generation to the next. Schools help to pass it on. It centres upon moral values.

IV   Moral values must be taught, but without repressing individuality. Examples of great individuals. Individuality must be encouraged and the system must channel rebelliousness into creativity.

V   Social and individual must be balanced. The links between the two are curiosity and creativity. Curiosity, the key to originality, must be stimulated. The roles of curiosity and creativity defined. The extremes of rigid conformity and instability must be avoided by balance.

VI   Balance of physical and mental also: *mens sana in corpore sano*. By physical is meant health and sex education, and not only the individual's and the society's health but the health of the environment on a global scale.

VII   Balance is needed between arts and sciences.

VIII   In a word of rapid change, most subjects now need a global approach.

IX   These rapid changes mean morality lags behind: the new information technology collects the information but cannot make fast enough the increasing number of ethical decisions required.

X   'A race between education and catastrophe' (HG Wells). Education helps us make wiser decisions.

XI   The more immediate, vocational concerns of education must follow awareness of the larger purposes.

TASK 2

Rewrite the essay in approximately 1,000 words, taking account of the above analysis, criticism and suggestions. Think about the subject and come to your own conclusions. The important thing is that you analyse and argue well, readably and interestingly. Since the essay covers so much ground and has to deal largely with abstractions, you may prefer to narrow the theme down by focusing on the individual aspects, or the social, or on a key quality such as balance or curiosity, or on the preparation for employment, or you may want to give it a sociological or political context. You may find more room, if you narrow down the scope, to back up your points with examples.

Then compare the result with the version B given in Appendix E. This covers just as much ground as version A so that, whichever approach you take, comparison is likely to be useful.

SUMMARY

● There is not one 'correct' content or approach for an essay on a given topic. Essays with very different approaches may be equally satisfactory, especially with large, abstract subjects.

● Where definitions of key terms in the instruction may vary, be sure to make clear how your definitions of those terms and consequently your whole approach may differ from others.

11

How to Pass Your Exam Essay

TERM ESSAYS AND EXAM ESSAYS

Since the term essay is the result of studying a given topic, with plenty of time to write it up, expectations are higher than, and different from, those of exam essays. Compare the expectations:

The term essay should:
1. Deal with the topic fully.

2. Show wide reading.

3. Result from substantial knowledge of the topic, with original thinking.

4. Provide a logical, well-structured explanation/argument, honed after two or three drafts into a readable and convincing piece of work.

5. Have careful and clear presentation.

The exam essay should:
1. Deal with the topic as comprehensively as time permits.

2. Show that you have studied to effect the information supplied and the texts prescribed for the course.

3. Result from your having applied the knowledge gathered, with some originality.

4. Be as well structured and as well written as a first draft can be expected to be.

5. Be as clearly presented as possible, allowing for the necessary speed of working.

The exam essay can be anything from 300 words — if there are several to complete — to 1,000 words or more. This chapter will cover:

- preparing for your exam
- using a winning strategy
- writing quickly but well
- reviewing your answer.

PREPARING FOR YOUR EXAM

Your course outline as printed in a handbook or supplied by your tutor should make it clear what the exam is to cover. Check with your tutor that the exam to come will cover the ground indicated; check that the format of the exam will not differ from past papers, if these are available.

Look through any past papers to see how they are laid out, how much time is allowed, how many topics there are to deal with, what sort of questions are asked, which topics are likely to come up, and so on.

Your revision

There are three stages to revision: learn it, check it, apply it.

Learn it

First make sure that your notes for the course are complete. Do they cover all the ground that will be covered by the exam? Study past papers to see if your notes would adequately cover the points raised by the exam topics. Do any extra reading necessary to make notes to fill gaps.

Indicate sources (texts with page numbers) clearly. Go back to the texts to clarify any notes you don't understand. Put your notes in order. You may want to highlight the main points of notes that are not included on your cards. Read through your completed notes two or three times.

Check it

Check that the forthcoming exam will follow the format of the most recent one. Check each section of your notes by putting them away and writing a summary of the main points, then comparing. Add anything missed. Ask a fellow-student to check whether you can repeat main points verbally.

Apply it
Complete from your notes one or two plans for topics of past papers, and complete one or two essays from the papers without referring to the notes, under exam conditions. Keep to the time allowed, and use notes for this practice only if they will be allowed at the exam.

If mock exams are arranged for you, they may be sufficient. Check with your tutor.

USING A WINNING STRATEGY

It's a good idea to experiment with different exam strategies when working through past papers to find out which suits your subject, needs and temperament. Here is some general advice, on choosing and timing, and on planning your answers, from which you can select what works for you.

Choosing and timing
First read through all the instructions and questions/topics. How long will you have for each? Allow five or ten minutes for the planning of each topic, and ten minutes at the end for revision.

Which topic or topics will you deal with? Choose carefully. Allocate a sheet of paper for your notes, plans and any other rough work. On this sheet immediately jot down any points, dates, figures, quotes, references under each topic title chosen.

Planning your answers
Look through Chapter 4 again and remind yourself of the different kinds of essay patterns and plans. Consider these three kinds of plans and choose the most suitable for each topic chosen: **a basic plan, a linear-logical plan**, and **a mind map**.

A **basic plan** might involve little more than underlining the key terms and making a note or two on each, or a few lines summarising what you will say. You may want to make a basic plan for all chosen topics before you start on any of the essays. The advantage of this is that you will then be able to flesh out a last topic quickly if you are running out of time towards the end. It is better to provide an outline in note form for your last topic, at least covering the main points, than a hotch-potch of undigested material put together in a panic.

- The **point-per-paragraph** plan described on pages 57–59 is particularly useful for the short essay, say 300 words, with three or four paragraphs. For longer essays you can adapt: two or three paragraphs for each main point.

- You may find **mind maps** better planning tools in exams. They may get your mind working more quickly and creatively: the required knowledge may be more speedily summoned and applied to the task in hand.

- **Conclusions** tend to be especially important in exams. You may find that a sentence or two of conclusion at the end of each plan will keep you firmly on the track at the writing stage. Put in any links between points that occur to you as you plan.

WRITING QUICKLY BUT WELL

The key to writing quickly and well is to **keep calm**. You should be able to keep calm if you revised methodically and effectively and have now made sure that your plans, however brief, do cover the main points required by the topics.

Before launching into the writing stage, check that you feel calm. If you find yourself tense, relax your muscles and take a few deep breaths. Do this several times during the exam.

Don't panic. You may feel that you've forgotten almost everything or even that your mind will go blank. Many students feel this way at the start of an exam. Examiners will look for substance in your exam paper rather than elegance. The fact that it has to be a first draft is taken into account. Don't confuse reassurance with complacency though. Once your pen is flowing, the ideas will flow too.

Dealing with writer's block

Techniques for dealing with writer's block during a term essay were described in Chapter 5 (see pages 65–67). Discover which of these techniques you could adapt during exam essays, when writer's block may be a more serious problem. If you practise the more likely techniques during your revision period, you can reassure yourself that you will be able to use them if necessary during an exam.

- Making a **mind map**, or adding to one you're already using, may get the writing flowing again. A simple planning device such as the People and Perspectives formula (page 53) may work.

● If you are unable to finish a topic within the time you've allowed yourself, **begin a new paragraph** (so that you will be able to continue), leave plenty of space to complete it, and go on to the next topic. You are likely to get more marks for two half-completed essays than for one completed, however good that is, for giving it more time than it deserved.

Linking as you go

The essay on education at Appendix E might well have been an exam essay. Whatever its shortcomings, notice that among its virtues there is a crucial one: it is concise and well linked up.

Achieve conciseness by linking as you go, and avoid digressing.

REVIEWING YOUR ANSWER

Even if you have only five minutes at the end to review your exam, you may be able to add marks by eagle-eyed editing. As you read through, check the following:

1. Are there any errors in grammar, spelling, punctuation, word usage, facts, figures, quotes, quotations?

2. Does the essay deal satisfactorily with the topic?

3. Look closely at the introduction and conclusion. Do they both directly and convincingly address themselves to the topic?

4. Is there a chain of explanation/argument, made clearly visible by links and related terms?

5. Is there a clear logical order in the arrangement, chronological where necessary?

6. Are opinions backed up by facts, and arguments by supporting evidence?

Appendix A
The Tasks: Suggested Responses

CHAPTER 1

Neil

Neil learns that the purpose of an argument essay is to persuade, and that the introduction should indicate clearly the writer's aim. Persuading means at least recognising the opposing point of view. Any argument should be backed up by some supporting evidence.

Marjorie

Marjorie learns that to indicate character development in a literature essay, when there is a lifetime to choose from, requires picking out the chief ('crisis') points. The title gives the first and last stages in Celie's development: Marjorie has to find the others and link them in her account.

Walter

Walter learns that the purpose of a how-to essay is to leave the reader with a clear idea of what to do, why it is being done, and in what order to do it. Planning it carefully is therefore essential. A report rather than essay format might be acceptable.

CHAPTER 2

1. (a) *'Wisdom* is *wasted* on the *old'*. How far do you agree with this statement?
   The instructional words are: 'do you agree?'

   (b) Paraphrase: give the arguments for and against the proposition that by the time we have acquired the knowledge and experience to live sensibly and fruitfully, physical and mental decline prevents us from making the most of that knowledge and experience. (Such a generalisation will need careful definition of the key terms.)

2. (a) Why were Allied Forces able to make *rapid progress* in their North African *campaigns* of 1942-3 but *slow* to make *progress* in their Italian campaigns of 1943-5?
    The instructional phrase implied is: 'explain why . . .'

    (b) Paraphrase: explain why the Allied Forces' military operation in North Africa in 1942-3 achieved their objectives more quickly than did their operations in Italy, 1943-5.

3. (a) What may be the *effects* of an *increase* in *leisure time*?
    The instructional words implied are: 'speculate on' . . . 'give your opinion on . . .'

    (b) Paraphrase: give your opinion on the likely changes that will take place when people spend less time earning their living. How will this increased leisure time affect, for example, the way society is ordered, its institutions, and the way people live and work?

4. (a) Examine the *significance* of Brutus's *role* in Shakespeare's *Julius Caesar.*
    The instructional word is 'examine'.

    (b) Paraphrase: assess how important the character and behaviour of Brutus is to the working out of the action of the play: their influence on the main events and themes and on the other characters.

5. (a) Does the increasing *popularity* of *fringe religious groups* indicate that *secularisation* is a *myth*? A-Level Sociology May 1993 (Oxford).
    The implied instructional words are 'argue for and against'.

    (b) Paraphrase: argue for and against the proposition, assessing the different ways commentators have been looking at 'secularisation' (the introduction of non-religious elements) and how these affect the way we look at religion as a whole. Assuming that cults and sects such as the Moonies are becoming more popular, explain how that popularity affects the way we view the notion of secularisation. (You might want to question the assumption, or place more emphasis than this paraphrase suggests on the various categories given to fringe religious groups.)

CHAPTER 3

After assessing the merit of your note-taking exercise with a quality paper leader, do a few more until you attain a good level of speed and accuracy.

CHAPTER 4

Detailed outline for the body of an essay. A likely arrangement is suggested below. For a term essay or coursework you would collect up to date information on the current state of research into dangers to health, figures on economic aspects, and so on, from such pressure groups as ASH (Action on Smoking and Health), the Royal College of Physicians, the Health Education Council and from those supporting the rights of smokers, manufacturers, and traders such as the Tobacconists' Association.

'How effective are the campaigns against smoking?'

I THE PUBLICITY AND THE LAW

1. Anti-smoking adverts now fairly effective. Number of smokers continues to decrease (?). Tar reduction *etc*.

2. No tobacco promotion broadcast: health warning required elsewhere: complete ban on media promotion possible.

3 Argument that complete ban unfair: allow it but tax it?

4. Tax plus revenue from sales — use for more Govt anti publicity?

5. Argumt that law agnst publicity and practice (in public places *etc*) must be stronger.

6. Cf with argt that stronger wld be unfair discrimn

(In II-IV each anti-smoking point and each line of argument to be related to the amount and effectiveness of publicity given to them in campaigns.)

II HEALTH

1. 5 mins less life for each cig? Other figs?

2. Addictns shld not be encourd.

3. But: less dangerous to self and others than other addictns less controlled (alcohol? tranquillisers?).

4. Life-threatg diseases: cancer of throat, bronchitis, emphysema.

5. Other dangers from tar, nicotine, carbon monoxide.

6. (Not only but also) dangers to others: foetus of pregt woman smoker.

7. Cf with pregt woman drinking alcohol.

8. Argts pro: reduces stress, induces relaxn, pleasure.

III ECONOMIC

1. High cost keepg ill smokers alive.

2. But revenue from sales for Govt; and cld tax adverts (see above).

IV HUMAN RIGHTS

1. Smokers make envirt unpleast: smells, *etc.*

2. Smokers also have rts not be branded anti-social.

3. Resrictns geny agreed, but individ rt to smoke must remain.

4. Bad example to children.

5. So incr health educatn? Decr harmfulness of tobacco?

CHAPTER 5

Comment

The passage is wordy, with little order, one sentence suggesting the next. What add to the confusion are the frequent changes of subject:

> I . . . reasons . . . other people . . . social reasons . . . smoking . . . survey . . . attitudes . . . it . . . smoking . . . people . . .

The reasons why people smoke are said to be, in this order:

> socialising . . . pleasure . . . relaxation . . . habit . . . relaxation . . . stimulation . . . socialising . . .

The reasons repeated need to be brought together. A better order is probably: socialising, pleasure, relaxation and stimulation, habit (most important last).

For clarity the points should be stated, and then discussed, in the same order.

Suggested rewrite

Smokers have four main reasons for smoking. The first is to be sociable. When smokers were more numerous, smoking helped you to make friends and to make social occasions go smoothly. Now that smoking has become widely anti-social, other reasons have become more important. Secondly, smoking brings pleasure. Thirdly, it is stimulating. It helps smokers to relax at moments of stress and after hard work, and it keeps them interested and cheerful. Smoking, however, is addictive and for long-term smokers the main reason must be the craving for nicotine.

(93 words)

CHAPTER 6

A

1. Eileen told Mary, the receptionist, that Bridget, the manageress, was upset by the remarks that Eileen had made to Bridget. (*It is better to be boringly inelegant than quite unclear.*)

2. (*Make two sentences.*) People having special qualifications or experience in race relations are being employed on their staffs by one or two of the largest local authorities. These new employees will work as certifying officers and advisers to the Race Relations Act committees.

3. Programme-budgeting must be flexible. (*Put the meaning into verbs where possible rather than nouns. 'Lynch-pins' is the wrong metaphor to refer to flexibility.*)

4. The road from A to B is not yet being built.

5. The New Scottish Nation Movement may not be sectarian, but it is playing into the hands of those who are. (*The original says the opposite of what it intends to say. Be careful with negatives.*)

6. It was assumed that it was not too important for candidates for selection to have polished manners. Some people objected to this policy.

7. This company aims to get the message across rather than stimulate the imagination.

8. The operator increased the machine speed by pressing the pedal. (*Verb rather than noun, active rather than passive.*)

9. They were extremely short-sighted to agree to the recommendation of the local council department.

10. What Henry VIII said was certainly not true.

CHAPTER 7

1. The selection of facts is unfair in this criticism of British culture. No doubt the USA and Norway have their own versions of Who wants to be a Millionaire? The statement makes a serious point effectively, however, and what follows can show that exaggeration is intended. More suitable, though, for a newspaper article than an essay.

2. Comment similar to that made for number 1.

3. Too sweeping. 'Inevitably' is overcharged.

4. The credibility of the argument suffers, however many facts are drummed up for evidence, because it is an argument that has been repeated by the old or the secure from the time of Adam. What follows will be convincing only in so far as it makes specific points about the special kind of rebellion of youth today and about the particular causes today.

5. This begs the question: the writer has a mind already made up and is not open, on this evidence, to other opinions. Clues to this attitude are the emotive use of the words 'thought up', 'proved', 'restore'. Whatever it was that made Britain great, I don't think the view that it was educational standards would be easy to support.

6. Sweeping generalisation. On the contrary, most single mothers are some years older than teenagers and are not in need of a home. Facts have been selected to support a political attitude to a social problem, conveniently ignoring the facts that don't.

7. Sweeping generalisation with emotive language ('all its works'). It is unwise to insult people of the opposite view so blatantly, when a convincing argument depends on confronting that view. 'Freedom' is a notoriously misused word, since one group losing freedom may mean another gaining it, and that switch may be justified. The greater freedom of choice when choosing food that has followed from EU regulations requiring manufacturers to list ingredients on containers is going to be ignored. Such terms as 'obviously' and 'as is well known' are more likely to irritate the reader than to win the reader over.

8. False syllogism. The assumption of the major premise is wrong.

9. Begs the question. The example of newspapers giving too much attention to TV celebrities will stand up better if it is followed up by an analysis that shows the proportion to be unjustified.

10. A similar comment to that for number 9, on the opposing viewpoint. Both arguments will gain credibility if they go on to confront the other side.

11. False syllogism. The middle sentence is called the 'undistributed middle' because it doesn't relate to the third. The conclusion is based on the assumption that all four-footed animals are dogs, which is not true, and is quite different from saying that all dogs are four-footed.

12. (b) is correct. This is like number 11. Choosing (a) would be indulging in the 'all-for-some' fallacy (see pages 91-92).

13. Assuming it's true that more children die from vaccination than from smallpox: this doesn't establish the conclusion because more people are vaccinated than exposed to infection or develop small-pox. What is required is to compare those not vaccinated who died from smallpox with those vaccinated and exposed to infection who did not develop the disease.

CHAPTER 8

(A) Introduction to 'How equal are the women in the Armed Forces?'

Thinking of the Armed Forces today doesn't immediately make you think of women. Images of brave men, in aeroplanes, ships or tanks will be recalled, as seen on television. When women do come to mind, you are likely to see them as nurses, secretaries and in the other supporting roles traditionally associated with women. Yet in recent years, reflecting their faster progress in civilian life, women's prospects in the Armed Forces have improved, with much integration and many more occupations open to them.

The view is still widely held, however, both inside the Forces and out, that war is a man's game, and that women get in the way. This essay will discuss those influences that keep women back in the Forces, with special emphasis on the issue of combat. Experience of combat is necessary for the top jobs, and keeping women out of combat has therefore a discriminatory effect, however much it is claimed that it does not.

(159 words)

(B) Conclusion to the same essay

Unfairness, therefore, remains. There is a chance that redefining of the term 'combat' will affect the issue. The Geneva Convention considers all military personnel as combatant. It is difficult to maintain the old distinctions. More non-combatants — called 'civilians' — have been killed in the wars since 1945 than soldiers. Furthermore, much killing in modern wars is done by remote control: consider the woman aircraft-controller who helps the pilot to destroy his target. The more the distinction is eroded, the more equal women will be.

(87 words)

CHAPTER 9

(a) LIFT EMERGENCIES. If the alarm bell rings or if someone is trapped in the lift, please telephone . . .

(b) You ask if you can put on the club noticeboard a leaflet about establishing an Amateur Dramatic Society. Please let me know who produced the leaflet and who authorised it. I wonder if the notice board is the right place for it.

(c) Further rebellions followed in Cornwall and Norfolk during Edward VIII's reign. A weak and sickly child, Edward had a Regent to rule on his behalf.

(d) Willy Loman, the protagonist, is certainly responsible for much of the unhappiness, mainly because he had deluded himself that he would be successful as a travelling salesman, and had deceived his two sons about what success required. He was in fact a failure — inattentive and inconsistent, and clearly heading for a breakdown.

He had brought his sons up to believe that the American Dream was theirs for the asking. All you had to be was self-confident. Well-meaning, he had only made them equally delude themselves. When his deceptions were exposed, the sons blamed him for their unhappiness and had little sympathy for him. Their mother supported him to the end, declaring 'Attention must be paid to such a man'.

(121 words)

CHAPTER 10

Task 1

A climax order (less important to more important) seems preferable, ending with the prospect for world peace. Numbers 3 and 6 need to be consecutive. The result: 2, 5, 3, 6, 1, 4. Discuss with a fellow-student or your group the advantages and disadvantages of other orders.

Appendix B
Note-Taking Sample

The following extract is from G M Trevelyan, *Illustrated English Social History, Vol. 4: The Nineteenth Century*, Pelican Books, 1964, pp 31-33 (first published by Longmans, Green, 1942). The note-taking in the margin assumes that all the main points are needed. All headings have been added.

THE DECLINE OF THE VILLAGE IN THE EARLY 19TH CENTURY

1. Population move to town or abroad:
(a) move to London with easier travel, recorded 1771
(b) now to other towns, espec. N, to industries (census figs 1801-31 show popn decr)
(c) Avge Eng village showed stable popn but many y.g. left for towns or abrd

As far back as 1771 Arthur Young had deplored the fact that, with better facilities of travel, the drift of country lads and lasses to London was on the increase. But now other towns were also drawing away their thousands from all parts of rural England. The movement was most marked in the north, the region of mines and factories and cotton mills. Indeed, the census figures for 1801 to 1831 show that some outlying parishes in the north were already diminishing in population every decade. This was not yet true of the average English village; but although a rural parish in the first thirty years of the century might show no drop in the number of its resident inhabitants, it was none the less sending many of its young people to the colonies or the United States, or to the centres of industry and commerce at home.

The continual rise in the population

2. Manufactg
industries
moved to town:
(a) incr popn
causg unemplt
(b) vill → purely
agric
(c) trad industries
moved to town

3. Self-suffy
eroded:
(a) easier travel
encourd. shoppg
in town
(b) new 'vill shop'
sold town/
overseas gds
(c) crafts
died out

(d) country life
slowly bec.
dependent
and dull

made it indeed impossible to provide work for everyone in the English village. Agriculture had absorbed all the hands it required. And many traditional kinds of rural occupation were disappearing. Great national industries, like cloth, were migrating back out of the country districts to which they had moved in the later Middle Ages and Tudor times. The village was becoming more purely agricultural; it was ceasing to manufacture goods for the general market, and, moreover, was manufacturing fewer goods for itself.

With the improvement of roads and communications, first the lady of the manor, then the farmer's wife, and lastly the cottager learnt to buy in the town many articles that used to be made in the village or on the estate. And a 'village shop' was now often set up, stocked with goods from the cities or from overseas. The self-sufficing, self-clothing village became more and more a thing of the past. One by one the craftsmen disappeared — the harness-maker, the maker of agricultural implements, the tailor, the miller, the furniture-maker, the weaver, sometimes even the carpenter and builder — till, at the end of Victoria's reign, the village blacksmith was in some places the only craftsman left, eking out a declining business in horseshoes by mending the punctured bicycle tyres of tourists! The reduction in the number of small industries and handicrafts made rural life duller and less self-sufficient in its mentality and native interests, a backwater of the national life instead of its main stream. The vitality of the village slowly declined, as the city in

a hundred ways sucked away its blood
and brains. This century-long process
had already begun between Waterloo and
the Reform Bill.

Summary

The decline of the English village in the early 19th century accompanied
a population move to the towns or abroad. The move to London, with
easier travel, had been recorded as early as 1771. The census figures for
1801 to 1831 show a population decrease in Northern villages as people
moved to the towns in the region, to the industries there. Although the
average English village showed a stable population, many young people
left for towns or went abroad.

The manufacturing industries of the country were returning to the
towns and the general increase in population meant unemployment in
the villages, which were becoming purely agricultural. Their self-
sufficiency was slowly eroded as people were encouraged by easier
travel to shop in town. Some goods manufactured in towns and abroad
were sold in villages, the country crafts died out, and country life
became dependent and dull.

Appendix C
Detailed Outline for an Essay

(For Appendices C and D, Fowley Borough Council, London, and one of its housing estates, The Downs View Estate, and the Cooperative Community Trust, a charity that sponsors various community projects, have been specially created.)

Topic: How successful have recent housing policies of London boroughs been in improving 'dump' estates? Back up your discussion by giving examples of the defects and improvements of at least one typical estate.

I INTRODUCTION

1. Definitions: 'dump': putting the most disadvantaged into the worst housing; 'disadvantaged': most unstable among the homeless, people from slum clearances, poorest, unemployed, *etc.*

2. The problem: defects of dump estates likely to get worse.

3. Solutions: more socially sensitive allocations since mid 70s.

4. But old pattern of disadvantaged persists.

5. The recession of late 80s: many ideas but lack of money.

6. Why the Downs View Estate, the example used throughout, is typical.

II THE RISE OF THE 'DUMP' ESTATE

1. Why council tenants tend to be disadvantaged.

2. Why council tenants on worst estates tend to be most disadvantaged.

3. Housing policies often insensitive:

    (a) 'Hard to let' housing allocated more quickly by making it single-offer.

    (b) Therefore policy ensured it went to most desperate, *ie*, most disadvantaged and most unstable.

    (c) More socially sensitive policies in mid 70s, but effects of dumping persist.

    (d) Since late 80s recession, lack of cash = housing policy regression.

III THE PATTERN OF DECLINE

(Defects generally widespread: specific points refer to Down View Estate)

1. Architecture encouraging vandalism and noise:

    (a) Low-rise blocks with long internal corridors, saving money on stairways, balconies, *etc*.

    (b) Difficult to check on non-residents' use.

    (c) Lack of natural light, dark stairways on corners.

    (d) Thin walls, loud music.

    (e) Lack of play area: children vandalise.

    (f) Inadequate rubbish disposal: dogs, mice, cockroaches, ants, *etc*.

    (g) Dog mess, *etc*.

2. Breeding ground for crime.

    (a) Effects of unemployment, instability, *etc*.

    (b) Many children: from delinquency to crime.

    (c) Long corridors, various entrances and exits.

    (d) Vicious circles: more burglaries — more dogs — increasingly unattractive estates — more disadvantaged tenants . . .

IV CONFLICT RATHER THAN COOPERATION

1. Young against old.

2. Victims against parents of delinquents.

3. Pet-owners against non-pet owners.

4. Rent payers against squatters.

5. Combinations of above.

V IMPROVEMENTS PLANNED BUT ABORTED BY LACK OF MONEY

1. Increase of number of stairways (very expensive).

2. More secure doors and windows.

3. Entry phones.

4. Gardens, within better landscaping.

5. Play facilities.

6. More lighting.

7. Repair of lifts.

8. New draining system.

9. New rubbish disposal units.

10. Improvements completed: Secure windows, painting, more lighting, start on play area.

VI DEVELOPMENT OF TENANTS' ASSOCIATION

1. Recent development, but then decline.

2. Sense of community increased, but much of this lost.

3. Meetings with council housing officers, estate manager, *etc*, organised by Cooperative Community Trust in 2-year housing action project:

    (a) small increase only in tenants' attendance;

    (b) some increase in articulateness: help for writing letters, reports;

    (c) disillusionment: lack of action.

VII CONCLUSION: ROOM FOR OPTIMISM

1. Hopes for more money for improvements in due course.

2. But social make-up of dump estates unlikely to change quickly or much.

3. Advice and assistance on estates more accessible.

4. In the long term, social inequalities in society in general need to be removed: these inequalities at most glaring on dump estates.

Appendix D
Detailed Outline for a Report

REPORT ON A TENANTS' ASSOCIATION

The title page

THE TENANTS' ASSOCIATION OF THE DOWNS VIEW ESTATE
FOWLEY BOROUGH COUNCIL, LONDON

Report on the Cooperative Community Trust's housing action project to build the moribund association into an effective pressure group, influencing the way the council's planned improvements to the estate would be made: January 1990- December 1992.

By James Maxton and Shirley Waites, Project Workers
6.1.93

Contents list

As for the Contents pages of this book. Many reports would follow this kind of division. The numerical system of division commonly used in reports is used here for the sake of contrast.

The body of the report

1. **TERMS OF REFERENCE**

   1.1 The project, sponsored by the Cooperative Community Trust, a charity organisation, was begun on 1.1.90 and terminated on 31.12.92.

   1.2 The two project workers collaborated with the following housing officers of Fowley Borough Council, . . . the Estate Manager, Mr Norman Willis, J. P. Latham Architects Plc, and the following members of the Downs View Tenants' Association Action Committee . . .

1.3 The report is distributed to the above list.

1.4 The objectives of the two-year project were as follows: to describe the defects and problems in the estate at the start of the project, to discover the causes of the decline in the previous five years or so, to give an account of previous tenants' associations that failed to survive, to show how the moribund association was revived, to give an account of the improvements to the estate achieved by the end of the project, and to conclude by making recommendations.

2. SUMMARY AND RECOMMENDATIONS

Some improvements were made to the estate but social make-up and indifference to tenants' association's work were little changed at the end.

It is recommended that the community workers' advice centre, monitoring the association's work, be kept on permanently, and that the council's housing policy should aim at widening the range of new tenants.

In the longer term substantial improvements will only come from greater equality for disadvantaged groups in society as a whole, and from their greater desire to act politically.

Sections 3 to 7 would expand on the points made in the Terms of Reference (1.4) in the same order, and the Conclusion (section 8) would expand on the Summary and Recommendations. The points can be picked out from the essay outline (Appendix B).

3. DEFECTS AT START OF PROJECT

4. CAUSES OF RECENT DECLINE

5. ABORTIVE TENANTS' ASSOCIATIONS

6. REVIVAL OF THE TENANTS' ASSOCIATION

7. IMPROVEMENTS TO ESTATE BY END OF PROJECT

8. CONCLUSION

The style of the report would remain as objective as possible, while the essay would be required to argue a point of view persuasively.

Appendix E
Rewriting of an Essay

VERSION B

WHAT IS EDUCATION FOR?

(This version of the essay was produced by the student who wrote version A, after taking account of the commentary on it at Chapter 10 — and two more drafts. It is not intended as a model for Task 2, but as a competent attempt at improvement.)

I think the philosopher Herbert Spencer expressed it best, certainly most concisely. He said, 'Education has for its object the formation of character.' Clearly in a general way, education must prepare us for life: it continues throughout our lives, it helps us to develop into mature human beings, in the widest possible sense. This essay will concentrate on formal education at school and university. I believe its purpose is, or should be, to help us to develop the character and skills to live at peace and earn our living in the society we find ourselves in. I believe the key quality to acquire for this is balance. Balance of social and individual, balance of physical and mental, balance of arts and sciences.

The educational system must prepare us to be effective both socially and individually. They are inseparable, but let's treat them separately for convenience. Socially, we have to learn to sacrifice immediate self-interest for the good of the greatest number, in other words learn how to socialise, in the widest sense learn how to be civilised, how to cooperate with others at work and at play. Individually, we have to learn to be ourselves, how to nurture our individuality, how to think for ourselves, and how to make as original a contribution to life as we are capable of.

How to thrive both socially and individually is what each generation teaches the next, and the most important subject of their lessons is moral values, whether in a religious framework or not. The schools help to pass on this inheritance in a formal way, and generally put the moral lessons into the framework of religious studies.

Teaching moral values should not require the repression of individuality. The educational system must recognise that many great men and women were rebels or dropouts in their school days. Winston Churchill, Britain's inspiring Prime Minister during the Second World War, and renowned author, didn't take to school. The list of the largely self-educated famous is long. Adolescents need to rebel to some extent against the expectations of society, and schools should recognise that this is a healthy part of growing up. A good educational system should be flexible enough to channel these rebellious instincts into creative and constructive channels.

The best system will balance the two. A system too concerned with the social or societal aspects of learning will send into the world, so to speak, too many bland, conventional people and too few people likely to take man's discoveries forward. Directing learners' attention outwards, imposing the targets on which those attentions must be directed, is more 'putting in' than 'drawing out' — and the emphasis should be on the latter in education; after all, that is what the word means. Emphasising the putting in represses and devalues curiosity and creativity, without which learning is mechanical and lifeless. Creativity in thinking comes from encouraging individuality. That creativity means the ability to analyse clearly and logically, come to your own conclusions and argue persuasively, avoiding the mere regurgitation of facts from notes and textbooks. A system over-concerned with encouraging individuality, on the other hand, will encourage unstable individuals and unstable societies.

As well as balancing social and individual, the system should balance physical and mental. By 'mental' is meant both intellectual and psychological. Individually this means fostering 'mens sana in corpore sano' (a sound mind in a sound body) as the ancient Romans used to say. It means not merely getting plenty of fresh air (to oxygenate the brain) and exercise at outdoor games and in the gym. It means attention to health education generally. Socially, health education includes putting sex education into the context of love, reproduction, marriage and long-term family commitments. Health education includes learning how to avoid drugs on an individual level, and how pollution of the environment should be avoided on a world-wide level.

An education that balances different disciplines — among the arts and the sciences — is also wanted. Curiosity in both areas should be stimulated, and there should not be too narrow specialisation too early. For the world becomes increasingly fast and complex, and the experience of living in it increasingly fragmented. A well balanced, well integrated educational system needs to help us understand this world.

It is a world in which we need more knowledge and more skills, in which change comes at an accelerating pace. Most subjects need a global approach rather than a national one nowadays. For example, a country's trade, and its economy, and its history cannot be understood except in a global context. We should learn at school, therefore, how nations are interrelated in their various pacts and international organisations. We should learn how multicultural, multiracial societies can operate harmoniously.

Education has to be constantly adapting to these changes. In some ways new technology has made the learning process easier: computers, for instance, have taken the tedium out of the gathering and processing of information. In other ways, new technology has created new problems for education to deal with. We cannot keep up with new discoveries: we cannot foresee how they will change our lives. Our understanding and our moral sense lag behind the knowledge and the skills acquired, for example in medical science. Thus there are numerous controversies to get embattled in: controversies about euthenasia, genetic engineering, and so on.

Our educational system must help us to make wise decisions in these areas. The destructive potential of nuclear power has to be balanced by the determination to create a world that can live in peace, and educationists have a large responsibility here. H G Wells's caution, many years ago in *The Outline of History*, is still forceful: 'Human history becomes more and more a race between education and catastrophe.'

More immediately, education is vocational, to help students to pass exams, and to prepare for careers that will suit their talents and special interests. But I have made the larger purposes the subject of this essay, because if there were no working towards them there would soon not be a world left to have a career in.

(1,000 words approximately)

In line with the instructions, this is the sort of creative essay that might fulfil the requirements of several disciplines for a warmer-up in the early part of a course, before the prescribed texts have been read. If the topic had been set to test knowledge at a later stage in a Sociology or Political Theory class, there would be discussion of such matters as how fair the schools were in promoting equality of opportunity. Mention would be made of the 'hidden agenda' to maintain the inequalities of class that Marxists see behind the stated policy of equality, and of the political implications of that theory in Government support of an independent education system, and so on.

At GCSE level, a more personal, free-wheeling approach would be acceptable in a creative essay on this topic.

Commentary

1. The confusing mix of pronouns in Version A is avoided by talking about the educational system when the discussion is general, and 'we' when the benefits are emphasised (except in the last paragraph which refers to the immediate benefits to current students). The advantage of 'we' is that it emphasises the fact that education continues throughout life. 'I' is used for the occasional signalling of the writer's chosen approach to the subject.

2. Bringing the Herbert Spencer quote to the start makes it more attention-grabbing.

3. Each paragraph is linked to the preceding one in ways described fully elsewhere in the book. Because it's a mainly abstract discussion, much use is made of repetition of key terms to achieve unity and coherence: 'education', 'balance', 'individuality', 'world', and so on.

4. The introduction — the first paragraph — makes the purpose and scope of the essay clear, and does it as concisely as possible. The conclusion rounds the essay off by referring back to the purpose and approach decided on.

Appendix F
Guide to Presentation

GENERAL

Any special/unusual kinds of presentation required for essays in a particular course will be indicated by your tutor. If you are in any doubt about how work should be presented, ask your tutor. This appendix illustrates the main requirements for essays in higher education. Up to A-Level, the requirements in some courses may be slightly less demanding, while for some university courses it may be necessary to refer to a more comprehensive guide, such as Kate Turabian's or Ralph Berry's (see Bibliography). Essays completed as parts of exams are of course not expected to contain detailed references.

1. From GCSE level onwards, spelling, grammar and punctuation should be correct, and if not, the essay will lose marks. There are some odd references in recent study guides suggesting that these elements are treated leniently. This attitude has changed since a decline in standards began to be deplored by university lecturers and employers, widely publicised in the media. The National Curriculum levels expect a reversal of the trends.

    Poor presentation of written work, whether related to the language, legibility, layout or general appearance, is equivalent to bad manners. Not only are examiners more kindly disposed to well presented work, it tends to be superior in other ways to poorly presented work.

2. Whether handwritten or typed, leave wide margins at the top, bottom, and on both sides of the page. This is to leave room for tutor's corrections and to make the essay easy to read.

3. Typescripts should be double-spaced, typed on one side of the page only.

4. A title page may be asked for. This will contain:

- The full title of the essay.
- The title of the course.
- The name of the teacher/tutor/lecturer.
- Your name.

(Other requirements for a title page may be indicated by a tutor, such as date of submission.)

STYLE FOR REFERENCES IN THE TEXT

The following is the commonly accepted style.

1. **Titles of newspapers, magazines, journals and books are underlined**. For example, in that order: <u>The Observer</u>, <u>History Today</u>, <u>British Medical Journal</u>, <u>The Making of the English Working Class</u>.

    Scholarly essays that need several references to books and articles in journals and magazines **normally give author and year of publication in the text**, to be followed by complete details in the Bibliography. Page numbers may be given in the text, or in the Bibliography. See Samples of References section below. If there are one or two such references only they may be given in full in the text, and a Bibliography at the end may not be expected.

2. **Articles** in newspapers, magazines, journals, encyclopedias, chapters or sections in a book, **are set in quotation marks**, with title of publication underlined and date. To this the Bibliography reference (see below) will add the page number.

3. **Titles of plays, films, musical compositions, radio and TV programmes, and art works; and names of ships, aircraft and spacecraft are underlined**.

4. The following applies mainly to term essays. **Short quotations** from literary or academic works **are set in quotation marks, or if long they may be indented**. Follow this with the titles of the work (if that is not obvious) plus page number.

    Extracts from classical plays, such as Shakespeare, if the locations are crucial **may need act, scene, line numbers**. For example, in an essay on *Antony and Cleopatra* a student writes:

    'Antony foresees his troubles very early in the play. Hearing in Egypt of his wife's death in Rome he says:

I must from this enchanting queen break off.
Ten thousand harms, more than the ills I know,
My idleness doth hatch . . .' (l. ii. 129-131)

If indented as above, quotation marks are not needed. If the lines of a play or poem are few, they may be arranged like these: 'I looked upon the rotting sea,/And drew my eyes away;/I looked upon the rotting deck,/And there the dead men lay' (Coleridge, *The Ancient Mariner*, Part IV). The Shakespeare play is the topic of the essay containing the first extract, so the title did not have to be repeated. The second extract is from an essay on history, so the author is needed.

STYLE FOR REFERENCES IN A BIBLIOGRAPHY

'Britain asks for joint attack on Euro-fraudsters', John Carvel, *The Guardian*, 21 March, 1994 (article in newspaper)

Myers, Norman. 'The Tropical Forest and You', *Environment Now*, April/May, 1988, p.37 (article in magazine)

Davis, Fred (1959), 'The Cabdriver and his Fare: Facets of a Fleeting Relationship', *American Journal of Sociology*, 65: 158-65 (or Vol. 65, pp 158-65) (article in a journal)

Eversley, David and Bonnerjea, Lucy, 'Social Change and Indicators of Diversity', in Rappoport, R N, Fogarty, M P and Rappoport, R (eds), *Families in Britain*, London: Routledge & Kegan Paul, 1982, pp 83-84 (section/chapter of book)

Thomas, Donald, *A Long Time Burning: The History of Literary Censorship in England*. London: Routledge & Kegan Paul, 1969 (book)

SAMPLES OF REFERENCES IN AN ESSAY

The following extracts are taken from a degree course essay in Psychology by Debbie Hawes: 'In what ways are psychological approaches shaped by different models of the person?' (Open University):

'. . . research into the causes of depression has looked at the role of various neurotransmitters in the brain and the effects of drugs which boost or suppress these neurotransmitters (Fries, 1954; Willner, 1985).'

'. . . behaviourists look for rules governing schedules of reinforcement or shaping and extinction of behaviour. Research would be limited to scientific experiments, such as those of B F Skinner, using a 'Skinner box' to study reinforcement in animals (Roth, 1990, pp. 268-272).'

'Any therapy is limited to helping the individual to understand his own behaviour, such as Carl Rogers's 'person-centred' counselling (Rogers 1951, 1959, 1961).'

'Marsh's study of football hooliganism involved observation and interviews with many "hooligans" and his explanation for his behaviour was in terms of the social rules of the "hooligan" subculture (Marsh, 1978).'

Bibliography

Roth, I (1990). *Introduction to Psychology, Vol 1.* The Open University.

Fries, ED (1954). 'Mental depression in hypertensive patients treated for long periods with large doses of reserpine', *New England Journal of Medicine, Vol 251*, pp 1006-8. Described in Roth (1990), p 231.

Willner, P (1985). Depression — *A Psychobiological Synthesis*, New York: John Wiley. Described in Roth (1990), p 232.

Marsh, P (1978). *The Rules of Disorder.* London: Routledge & Kegan Paul.

Rogers, CR (1951). *Client-Centred Therapy*, New York: Houghton. Described in Roth, I (1990), pp 438-441.

Rogers, CR (1959). 'A theory of therapy, personality and interpersonal relationships as developed in the client-centred framework', in Koch, S (ed), *Psychology: A Study of a Science*, Vol 3, pp 184-256, New York: McGraw-Hill. Described in Roth, I (1990), pp 438-441.

Rogers, CR (1961). *On Becoming A Person: A Therapist's View of Psychotherapy*, London: Constable. Described in Roth, I (1990), pp 438-441.

Glossary

Note: Some of the following terms have different meanings outside the discussion of essay writing.

Analogy. Similarity of objects/processes otherwise dissimilar.

Analysis. Divide into elements in order to explain.

Anecdote. A true story used to illustrate a point.

Anti-climax order. From more important to less.

Antithesis. The objections that might be raised to a viewpoint.

Argue. Maintain by reasoning, prove, persuade.

Bias. Conscious distortion of the truth (as in propaganda); or unconscious, as when influenced by one's own viewpoint or state of knowledge when note-taking.

Bibliography. List of printed sources referred to in an essay, which the reader may want to follow up as suggestions for further reading.

Brainstorming. Experimenting in different ways with word and idea associations as a means of getting ideas.

Climax order. From less important to more, or from simple to complex, or from familiar to unfamiliar .

Connectives. Linking words and phrases.

Deduction. Reasoning from the general to the particular.

Discipline. Branch of learning, subject.

Edit. Correct, improve, clarify, add, reorganise, rewrite: any or all of these, and usually reduce.

Exposition. Piece of writing that explains.

Evidence. Testimony or facts tending to make for a conclusion; examples backing up statements in an essay.

Fallacy. Flawed argument.

Formulae. Rules, statements or principles relating to a discipline: expressed in figures and symbols in Mathematics and Science.

In depth. (Reading): studying a text closely, as slowly as necessary to understand it and critically judge it.

Induction. Reasoning from the particular to the general.

Jargon. (1) terms used in a profession/discipline that are not in common use

(2) gibberish or gobbledygook (the unclear language of bureaucracy).

Legwork. The most direct kind of information-gathering: attending an event to observe for yourself.

Linear-logical. (Plan): indicating the main ideas and subdivisions of a text or an essay in progress in a formal way, using numbers and letters (see Appendices C and D for examples).

Logical order. In an order that shows correct reasoning.

Parallelisms. Repeating phrase, sentence or paragraph patterns to achieve greater clarity.

Paraphrase. To put into your own words when note-taking.

Quotations. Literary references: reporting the exact words of writers or critics being discussed, or of famous sayings.

Quotes. Statements made by interviewees reproduced in an essay.

Random associations. Brainstorming technique that involves putting alongside a concept words picked at random from your mind or out of a dictionary.

Recall. Making a memory check at a particular stage of your reading (for example, at the end of a section or chapter); reproducing the main points orally or in writing.

References. Evidence for statements in the form of quotes, quotations or paraphrase of authors, usually giving author's name, title of article or book, page number, publisher, date of publication (see Appendix E). See also 'sources'.

Review. (1) returning to a text to add to your notes anything you may have left out

(2) reading through your own work — notes or essay — to check what editing is required.

Scanning. Reading a text, knowing what you are looking for and selecting those passages, ignoring the rest.

Schematic. (Notes or plans): another term for linear-logical (see above).

Skimming, or skim-reading. Quickly exploring what information a text might contain that might be of use in your essay.

Sources. (Information): origins (mainly printed) of information used in an essay, including those that need references.

Style. Your way of writing, adapted to the discipline of the essay topic but remaining as natural to you as possible.

Thesis. Your viewpoint, what you set out to prove.

Further Reading

Bowden, John, *Writing a Report* (How To Books Ltd)

Buzan, Tony, *Use Your Head* (BBC Books). The author is the originator of mind maps.

Evans, Mike, *How to Pass Exams Every Time* (How To Books)

Gowers, Sir Ernest, *The Complete Plain Words*. Revised by Sir Bruce Fraser (Penguin Books)

Hoffmann, Ann, *Research For Writers* (A & C Black)

Inglis, John and Lewis, Roger, *Clear Thinking* (NEC/Collins Educational)

Jones, Bill and Johnson, Roy, *Making the Grade: A Study Programme for Adult Students. Vol. 1: Reading and Learning, Vol. 2: Thinking and Writing* (Manchester University Press)

McClain, Molly and Roth, Jacqueline D., *Writing Great Essays* (McGraw-Hill)

Morison, Murray and Pey, Jim, *Writing Sociology Essays: A Guide for A Level Students* (Longman)

Phythian, B. A., *Teach Yourself Correct English* (Hodder and Stoughton)

Pirie, David B., *How to Write Critical Essays* (Methuen)

Redman, Peter *et al, Good Essay Writing. A Social Sciences Guide (*The Open University)

Rowntree, Derek, *Learn How To Study* (Macdonald)

Smith, Pauline, *Writing an Assignment* (How To Books)

Todd, Allen, *Finding Facts Fast* (Penguin Books)

Turabian, Kate L., *A Manual for Writers of Research Papers, Theses and Dissertations* (Heinemann)

Watson, George, *Writing a Thesis* (Longman)

Recommended dictionaries: The Concise Oxford Dictionary, The Chambers Dictionary, the New Collins Thesaurus in dictionary form.

Index